THE GREAT WHALE BOOK

Large humpback breaches off the coast of New Hampshire, displaying long flippers. (Herb Moyer photo)

THE GREAT WHALE BOOK

John Kelly
Scott Mercer
Steve Wolf

The Center for Environmental Education

Acropolis Books, Ltd./Washington, D.C.

Library of Congress Cataloging in Publication Data

Kelly, John E. (John Ellison), 1948-
   The great whale book.
   Bibliography: p. 116
   1. Whales. 2. Whaling 3. Wildlife conservation.
I. Mercer, Scott. II. Wolf, Steve. III. Title.
QL737.C4K43   333.95'9   81-14946
ISBN 0-87491-468-X (pbk.)   AACR2

Distributed by ACROPOLIS BOOKS LTD., Washington, D.C. 20009

The Great Whale Book

Published by the Center for Environmental Education
624 9th Street, NW
Washington, DC 20001

Net proceeds from the sale of this book are used to expand education programs, fight needless killing of marine animals, and support research and action to protect the ocean environment.

Book and cover design, Carter/Cosgrove & Company

Typography by General Typographers Washington, DC

Printed in the United States of America

Foreword

Since the successful publication of our first *Whalebook* in 1978, the number of WHALE PROTECTION FUND sponsors has grown by 50% and the slaughter of whales decreased 31%.

Interest in whales covers a spectrum of people, from those concerned with needless slaughter and threat of extinction to those consumed with the idea of interspecies communication. The subject of whales fascinates both the young and the old, from scientist to artist. The appeal of whales is universal and their plight a measure of the resolve of humankind to live in harmony with all living organisms of this water planet called Earth.

The Great Whale Book is a source book, teaching tool, and conservation manual. The book summarizes the 6000-year tradition in which whales have been inextricably bound with human life and culture, and which may hold the key to our own survival.

We hope this book will add to the reader's understanding of and concern for these magnificent creatures.

Thomas B. Grooms
Executive Director
Center for Environmental Education
WHALE PROTECTION FUND

(*Jane Gibbs photo*)

Joan. Stradanus inuent.
Phls Galle exud.

Preface

This book tells of the evolution of whales and whaling, the destruction of the great stocks by commercial whaling, and the struggle to save whales from extinction. We confine our story to the ten largest whale species, plus the popular orca or "killer" whale. The field guide, which describes these eleven species, is designed to make the book useful to whale-watchers.

Information for this book was drawn from many sources. In a sense, it is a survey course on the art, history, science and economics of whales. We hope it excites readers enough to pursue the subject further, and our bibliography will provide a good start for those who wish to do so. We also hope this survey communicates the sense of urgency we feel about protecting great whales. Much research needs to be done, and the effectiveness of educational and lobbying work on behalf of cetaceans requires strong public support. We hope *The Great Whale Book* helps build this support.

The Center for Environmental Education, through its Whale Protection Fund, commissioned us to write this book. Responsibility for its content rests solely with us, yet suggestions from many people at the Center and elsewhere helped shape the book at several points. Judith Hinds, Elliott Norse, and Jann Teeple-Hewes of the CEE staff offered valuable criticisms throughout the preparation of the book. Alan Havens' comments greatly improved the section on biology, and Irene Bartholomew of the University of New Hampshire helped smooth out several rough spots. Particularly helpful during the photo research were Alta Copeland (Smithsonian Institution); Jean Miller (Folger Library); Warren Seamans (MIT Museum); Nicholas Whitman (New Bedford Whaling Museum); and the staff of the Washington, D.C. office of Greenpeace. Sara Meade's stately cetaceans gave the field guide a distinction it might otherwise have lacked. Zane Carter and Ken Cosgrove went without sleep on countless nights to work similar magic with the entire book.

Finally, we cannot praise too highly the staff of the Complex Systems Research Center at the University of New Hampshire. Special thanks go to Clara Kustra, Gina Sipe, Mal Towne, and Diane Voyles. We are grateful for their skills and dedication.

J. K., S. M., & S. W.

Accurate information about the natural world was scarce during the Middle Ages and the Renaissance, and a virtual zooful of fictional animals roamed through the European mind. Whales ranked among the most terrifying creatures in this imaginary menagerie and inspired countless popular tales about sea monsters. In this 16th-century engraving, the crews of the threatened ships ring bells in an effort to pacify the gathering cetes and balenas.

Introduction

People often ask how anyone can worry about whales when the danger of nuclear holocaust looms larger with every political crisis and people die from starvation daily. Perhaps the best answer is that the effort to save whales from extinction is also the effort to stop the gross mismanagement and abuse of resources that now threaten every form of life on the planet — including humankind. The depletion of whale stocks by commercial whaling represents precisely the kind of resource management problem that humans must solve if we are to survive. In other words, saving whales is a crucial measure of our ability to save ourselves.

Whales are what is called a common resource. Unlike forests or mineral deposits, no one owns whales. Though they may occupy a nation's territorial waters in the course of their yearly migrations, the extended range of most species makes it impossible for any one nation or transnational corporation to maintain exclusive control. The International Whaling Commission, a multinational regulatory agency, is charged with managing whale resources. It has done a poor job. Although conservation is the Commission's primary goal, it has failed to prevent the depletion of one whale stock after another.

Whales are not the only common resource that suffers this way. Improvements in technology and the constantly rising demand for food spur heated competition for another common resource, fish. Yet, the very fierceness with which each nation scrambles to claim its share of world fish stocks "before it is too late" almost guarantees that the stocks will be used unwisely. Ultimately, fishing nations will find that it is "too late" for everyone.

Garrett Hardin calls this drama the "tragedy of the commons," and it is not confined to international resources like whales and fish. Our national resources also face depletion in the frantic pursuit of energy and economic growth. The expanding search for offshore oil threatens the productivity of the marine ecosystem and the fisheries that form an important part of our economy. Rising demand for wood products and minerals makes it increasingly difficult to protect wilderness areas from logging and mining operations, the rape of the landscape by clear cutting and strip mining.

Mismanagement of natural resources is tragic because it is unnecessary. When the International Whaling Commission was formed in 1946, the vulnerability of whales to overfishing was well known. In each subsequent year, the IWC's own scientists warned that quota reductions were necessary to maintain stocks at permanently productive levels. The Commission ignored the warnings. Stocks declined as predicted. Now it is necessary to stop commercial whaling altogether to give stocks time to recover.

Rational management based on scientific evidence offers an opportunity to use natural resources without depleting them. But the logic of western economics — and we include both capitalism and communism as they are practiced in most countries — militates against prudent resource use. Instead, the mindless pursuit of economic growth and expansion leads to shortsighted overexploitation. It is not the fisheries' capacity to feed an increasing global population that is in question, but humanity's ability to manage those fisheries without destroying them.

As another example, oil companies have consistently battled regulations requiring them to employ the best available technology to prevent pollution from offshore petroleum exploration. The barging of pollutants such as drilling muds and drill cuttings away from oil fields is expensive. The costs of barging and other

NASA *photograph of Earth (Africa and the Arabian peninsula are outlined at center and top).*

methods of protecting the environment show up on corporate balance sheets, but the benefits to marine ecosystems do not. Yet, when the environment is *not* protected, there are other costs to be paid. One effective way to disguise these other costs is to spread them out as widely as possible, often by using the easiest method of waste disposal. It is not simply that oil companies lack incentives to employ safer disposal methods; our economic system actually encourages them to reject such methods if the costs of disposal can be passed along to other sectors of the economy. So fishermen and residents of coastal states suffer the impact of oil development while oil companies reap profits made possible by sloppy waste disposal practices.

The conflict between short-term economics and long-term conservation lies at the heart of this and similar problems. It is increasingly clear that the world's oceans cannot sustain the adverse impact of ocean dumping and chemical pollution, which are rapidly destroying the marine ecosystem. Millions of tons of sewage, toxic chemicals, petroleum, and pesticides still flow through rivers into the oceans each year. Their deadly effects are well documented, and though their extent is not widely recognized, we are fast reaching a point beyond which nature cannot recover from them. If that happens and the oceans die, the future of humankind, along with all other life on Earth, will be grim indeed.

Saving whales strikes us as one very good way of addressing the related problems of resource depletion and environmental pollution. Whales are monitors of planetary health the way canaries once served to warn Welsh coalminers of toxic gas leaks. The canaries were sensitive to chemical changes in the atmosphere, and when they stopped singing, the miners knew they faced death unless they got out of the mines quickly. Whales may well be our planetary canaries, a measure of the threats to the planet's crucial life support cycles.

But there are other reasons for saving whales. They are extraordinary creatures, and it is important to call human attention to their characteristics.

Whales are believed to be highly intelligent. They have the largest brains on earth, and in some species the brain-to-body ratio — considered an important measure of potential intelligence — is second only to humans'. These animals may be capable of understanding chance, love, and logic. To destroy forever this special mental capacity would be a tragic, wasteful act.

Whales have complex social structures. They bear their young by copulation, gestation, and parturition like humans, and some species are known to be monogamous. They are gentle and playful. Their only major predators are humans, yet whales continue to show a remarkable affinity for humankind. From the time of the ancient Greeks, dolphins have been known to come to the rescue of drowning sailors and to engage children in gentle play. Yet, whales also seem able to judge human purpose and approach only those with good intentions.

Whales can communicate with each other. Several species of smaller whales, in the group we commonly call the dolphins, have demonstrated in experiments their ability to use sound to communicate. Scientists have been trying to establish communication with dolphins for several decades. Some consider this a matter of teaching dolphins to understand our language translated into sound frequencies appropriate to their aquatic medium. Others believe that we should try to decode their language. Perhaps the most promising approach is to try to establish communication through interaction, with human and dolphin participants developing a mutual language. Recent advances in teaching primates to communicate using sign language developed for deaf/mute humans suggests that dolphins, with their great mental capability, may be quite communicative — if we can find the right medium.

Whales seem to live an almost utopian existence. Food is plentiful, at least for the present, and were it not for human predation whales would roam the world's oceans unmolested. They spend a good deal of time in play, which is often sexual in nature, and they appear to have avoided such pitfalls of human society as caste, class, and war. In short, they seem to have learned how to live in peace, a lesson humankind would be well advised to study.

Whales are highly evolved creatures. Some people believe that they are equal to humans in this respect — perhaps our superiors. Because their forelimbs are flippers, whales lack the ability humans derive from their hands to manipulate tools and alter their environment. Some people argue that whales are, therefore, less sophisticated than humans, yet the human ability to build and create has also been the capacity to kill and destroy. Over millions of years, whales have developed the capacity to live peacefully within their environment. Against such a standard, humankind ranks low on the scale of evolutionary sophistication.

Whales occupy a critical niche in their ecosystem. Though we do not fully understand their role, we cannot assume that system equilibrium would continue unaltered if they disappeared. In fact, decimation of Antarctic whale stocks has already brought about significant changes in the Southern Ocean ecosystem. Scientists think that ecosystem stability is linked directly to species diversity, and they are wary of the consequences of reduced diversity through extinction of species. Because we do not know exactly what role great whales play in the marine ecosystem, we should question the changes we may trigger by depleting the stocks.

These are all good reasons for saving whales, and they explain why so many people are concerned. They should not be confused, however, with criteria for selecting certain species that shall be allowed to flourish while others are diminished or die. Just because bats, for example, are small and rather unattractive is no reason to exterminate them. Like whales, they have unique characteristics and an ecological role to play.

In fact, the extinction of any species is a significant loss to the biosphere. We cannot accept the argument that other forms of life must be destroyed to make room for expanding human populations, be it the snail darter for another hydroelectric dam or the perigrine falcon for another pesticide. Human arrogance attains rarefied heights in the suggestion that we deserve to dominate the planet simply because we have the power to do it. Beyond that, the idea that humans could survive wholesale extermination of "competing species" is sheer stupidity.

We need a new concept of our role in the biosphere, one that appreciates the limits and value of the earth's resources and regards humankind not as the planetary master standing at the apex of evolution, but as a cooperating cohabitant integrated with all living things. Simply, we are responsible for managing our affairs on this planet wisely. This concept has been called "stewardship," and as a path for humankind to follow it makes far more sense than the course that has brought us to the edge of planetary disaster.

Seen from outer space, the Earth is a fragile blue-green sphere of life in the void of the Universe. As far as anyone knows, it may be the only one. Humankind might conceivably establish contact with life outside planet Earth. Humankind might even develop ways to visit distant planets. We prefer to think that the motivation for such contact comes from the intelligence and curiosity of humans as a species — not because we so pillaged our own planet that we must escape to survive.

In 1968 when this NASA photograph was indelibly etched into our memories, the effort to save whales had just begun. The International Whaling Commission finally agreed to protect the blue whale, and even though protection for that species may well have come too late, it was a beginning. Scientists working in the Commission decided it was time to take their case to the public, and those of us who responded did so in a variety of ways. Some worked to reform the IWC from within; others physically placed themselves between whalers and their victims; most of us simply wrote postcards and sent money to the cause. We were possessed with a sense of urgency, a feeling that the planet's limited resources were being rapidly consumed. The NASA photograph, a single image, contributed to this changed perspective. It had given us, quite literally, a global view.

The power of this image was foreseen by Fred Hoyle, father of the "Big Bang" theory of universal origins. In 1948 Hoyle wrote, "Once a photograph of the Earth taken from outside is available, once the sheer isolation of the Earth becomes plain, a new idea as powerful as any in history will be let loose."

It is too early to say exactly what that idea is — historians will have to do that — but for many of us, the idea of stewardship feels appropriate in response to the sense of isolation, limitation, and fragility that is so easily evoked by this image of Earth. By working to preserve the great whales of this planet, we begin our stewardship with a significant action that will have effects far beyond the saving of these magnificent creatures.

Water rushes from the mouth of a humpback as it feeds off the New Hampshire coast. Note the "stovebolts" covering its head. (Herb Moyer photo)

Contents

Armor of baleen plates made by Eskimos on Alaska's Diomede Island. (Smithsonian Institution photo)

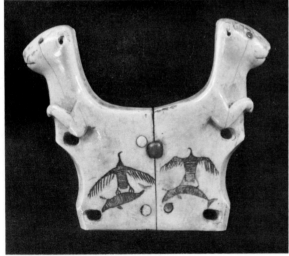

Whale line guide from Alaska. (Smithsonian Institution photo)

Like most aboriginal whale hunters of the North Pacific, Eskimos attached floats to their harpoons. These floats, made of wood or, as here, animal bladders, helped the hunters track the whale and eventually tired it out from the extra drag they added. When the hunters caught up with the exhausted whale, they killed it with more harpoons and lances. (Smithsonian Institution photo)

Whale Biology

Evolution

Over 345 million years ago, the first recognizable amphibian ancestor of the land vertebrates shook the mud and water from its body and climbed out on the banks of a lake or stream. As successive generations of the offspring of this animal spread across the land, they began to adapt to the various terrestrial environments they encountered. These "branches" continued to diverge: some died out, and one eventually became the ancestor of today's mammals.

Millions of years along in the course of this development, one group of mammals was drawn, very slowly, back toward the water and ultimately into the sea. Its members were the early ancestors of the great whales. We know little of the form or appearance of the ancestral cetacean — some scientists speculate that it resembled a rat or a weasel — but analyses of blood proteins have shown similarities between modern whales and the even-toed, hoofed mammals, such as camels, deer, and cattle.

Reconstruction of a whale ancestor (**Zeuglodon**) that swam over 20 million years ago in seas covering what is now the American Gulf Coast. (Smithsonian Institution photo)

The fossil record documenting this evolutionary U-turn begins about 45 million years ago. Three major groups of primitive cetaceans can be distinguished, including some great serpentlike creatures with jagged teeth. By the time the last of the archaic whales had disappeared about 20 million years ago, most of the modern groups of cetaceans had already developed.

The evolutionary forces behind the return of the ancestral whales to an aquatic environment remain unclear. Any of a number of factors may have been responsible: changes in habitat and food supply, predation, or the relative abundance of food near lakes, marshes, rivers, and in estuarine areas. Gradually, these ancestral whales became more successful in exploiting the food sources offered by the intertidal and marine habitats.

Dolphins, porpoises and whales all belong to the order **Cetacea**, which is further broken down into sub-orders of **Odontoceti** (toothed whales) and **Mysticeti** (baleen whales).

Two main distinctions divide the sub-orders. One is the presence or absence of teeth. Toothed whales include sperm and orca whales and all the porpoises and dolphins. The number of blowholes is the second distinction; toothed whales have only one.

The baleen group includes the remaining nine species examined in this book. In the upper jaws of these animals grow hundreds of strips of hard, flexible material called baleen, which is used to filter fish and plankton from the water. Most baleen whales have ventral pleats that allow their throats to expand while feeding. These pleats are missing in the two nonrorqual species. Baleen whales have two blowholes.

As in all species, new physical characteristics appeared by chance among the evolving cetaceans. Some of these changes made survival easier, helping the whales' ancestors swim faster, remain in cold waters for long periods, or dive farther under the surface. The offspring of the animals with these beneficial mutations were better suited to life in their environment and would have gradually replaced their less well-equipped cousins over millions of years.

While we cannot determine the order of the changes that took place, it is apparent that whale ancestors underwent cumulative modifications over millions of years until they became the cetaceans we know today. Fore and hind limbs changed as digits became interconnected with webbing. Individuals with webbing swam more efficiently and could dive farther and tread water more easily while catching their breath or feeding far from the shallows.

Reduction of fur was accompanied by changes between the muscle and the skin, where a thick layer of body fat slowly developed. This subcutaneous fat was a better insulator than a fur coat and may have hastened modification of the pelt and body. Hairs shortened and thickened, reducing drying time when the creatures came ashore and decreasing drag on bodies moving through water. Reproductive organs and mammary glands moved inside the body wall and away from exposure to cold water and air. Ultimately, the male sexual organs were exposed only during mating, and the females' mammary glands only during nursing.

Over time, the hind legs diminished, and the end of the slender tail flattened and widened. This reflected the direction of locomotion; instead of moving from side to side like that of a fish, the cetacean tail moved up and down on a vertical plane. The rear legs disappeared into the body wall and its thick layer of blubber. Today, most whales carry vestigial leg bones in the rear of their bodies.

Modifications of the rear half of the body produced a powerful tail that gave cetaceans the ability to move rapidly through the water. The forepaws were no longer needed for manipulating food as the cetaceans evolved mechanisms allowing them to overtake their prey and swallow it whole. Some cetaceans retained their teeth while others developed a sophisticated mechanism employing baleen which allowed them to strain their food from water rushing through their mouths. As the forepaws lost their food-catching role, they gradually became paddles or flippers adapted for maneuvering underwater.

A very important change involved the head. The body was becoming increasingly adapted to a horizontal posture for swimming. When the animal surfaced in this position, the top of the head would emerge first. This gave an advantage to animals with nostrils placed higher on their heads, and that benefit led to the gradual migration of the nose from the muzzle to the top of the skull. This allowed quick expulsion of spent breath and rapid intake of fresh air. The muscles around the nostrils thickened and strengthened, enabling the animal to pinch off the nasal openings upon submerging.

Perhaps the whales' most remarkable adaptation was the development of a navigational system suited to the marine environment. Because visibility is often limited in the ocean, eyesight was an unreliable means of locating food and preventing collisions with obstacles such as rocks or other whales. Cetacean ancestors that evolved an echolocation ability gained a major advantage in moving through dark and murky waters. Echolocation relies on sound waves beamed by whales into the water. The waves travel until they strike an object, bounce off, and return to the whale which can derive from them information about the object's size, location, rate of movement, and physical makeup. (Echolocation is discussed in detail later in this chapter.)

These North Pacific fur seals may share a
common ancestor with whales, but they
evolved in ways that suited them to life
both in and out of water. In addition to a
layer of body fat, their thick fur slows the
escape of body heat into the air. Thus, fur
was not lost during the course of seal
evolution. In contrast, cetaceans virtually
never leave the water. Hence, over millions
of years, they lost their fur and rely on
thick layers of blubber to conserve body
heat. (V.B. Scheffer photo, courtesy U.S.
Fish & Wildlife Service)

As a system for navigating in the marine world, echolocation offered advantages over sight and even the directional hearing that is so well developed in many land animals. Whales mastered the night sea as well as the dimly lit daytime ocean. They could hunt at depths beyond the reach of sunlight and in murky waters where mud and silt obscure even the closest objects.

In addition to echolocation, cetaceans evolved a remarkable ability to communicate vocally that allowed direct communication with companions, family members, and other species. Entire herds, sometimes of more than one species, could travel or hunt in coordination. Social structure gained a new sophistication as mammals with highly developed brains and group skills found their place in the seas.

Right whale blubber is thicker than that of any other great whale species. It can measure up to 50 cm (20 in). (Jane Gibbs photo).

Morphology and Physiology

Special physical adaptations are necessary for mammalian life to survive in the ocean. The shape of the body is one principal concern. A long, smooth form allows easy passage through the water. Whales have such a shape, tapering at the head and tail, with the bulk of the mass concentrated in the middle. The stouter whale species — the humpback, right, and bowhead — are often depicted as more blimp-like than they actually are. Although bulkier than their relatives, they are by no means ungainly. They could hardly survive in the ocean if they were. Whale streamlining extends even to smaller anatomical features. Sexual organs and mammary glands, for example, are tucked inside the body wall. This eliminates the potential drag they might add during swimming and keeps these essential organs warm and out of harm's way.

Maintaining warmth is a second major requirement for mammals living in the marine environment. The rate of heat transfer in the ocean is over twenty times greater than on land. Physiologists estimate that a human swimming in a 27-degree C (80 F) ocean loses as much heat as a human standing naked in a 7-degree C (45 F) room.

In adapting to the thermal demands of their environment, whales have evolved some unique features. Like all mammals, whales have three layers of skin. Sandwiched between the top two layers and the connective tissue covering the muscles is a blanket of fat known as blubber. This crucial insulating layer is characterized by a reduction in the number of blood vessels that would speed heat loss. Among the great whales, blubber varies in thickness by species. The sei whale has a relatively thin layer at 8-10 centimeters (3-4 inches). In blue and finback whales the blubber averages 10-15 cm (4-6 in); in humpback and sperm whales it is about 18 cm (7 in); and in right whales the blubber may be more than 50 cm (20 in) thick. These figures are averages, and exceptions are not unusual; for example, right whale blubber as thick as 70 cm (28 in) has been found.

Blubber works for a whale in three ways. First, as mentioned, it acts as an insulator that traps heat inside the whale's body. Many whale species feed in icy polar or sub-polar waters where this is particularly important, but even in the warmer tropical breeding grounds, ocean water can rapidly drain away body heat.

Blubber serves a secondary function as a storehouse of energy and nourishment in times of fasting or poor food supply. Breeding females build up a thick layer of fat while pregnant. As nursing of the newborn calf proceeds, the mother draws on the blubber to produce milk, and the blubber thins accordingly. The thickness of a whale's blubber layer varies with seasonal changes in environment and behavior. Blubber is thickest when a whale leaves the summer feeding areas for winter calving grounds. This sustains the whale for months in the breeding grounds where it may eat little or no food; the animal thins considerably by the time migration back to the summer feeding grounds begins. An exceptional example of this fluctuation is in blue whales, which can lose up to 36.3 metric tons (40 tons) in one season. Additionally, blubber aids movement through the water. The fat ripples when the whale swims, helping reduce drag on the body as it cuts through a medium that is 200 times thicker than air.

Even the absence of sweat glands demonstrates the whale's elegant adaptation to life in the ocean. Sweating helps land mammals stabilize their body temperatures through evaporative cooling; evaporation cannot occur under water.

Blubber is not the only feature that helps cetaceans maintain heat in the ocean. Temperatures on land may fluctuate up to 27 degrees C (80 F) in a 24-hour period.

Measurements in this book are given in metric terms, with rough English system equivalents following in parentheses. In some cases we have rounded the converted numbers to avoid long fractions.

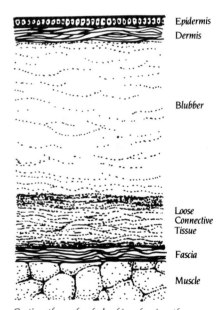

Epidermis
Dermis

Blubber

Loose Connective Tissue

Fascia

Muscle

Section through whale skin, showing the two upper layers, the insulating blubber, and the loose connective tissue attached to the muscle. The blubber is only sparsely supplied with blood vessels, a characteristic that increases its ability to retain body heat.

But in the ocean, daily temperature changes are slight, and one source of climatic stress is much reduced. In contrast to land mammals, which must be able to adjust their body temperatures to rapidly changing conditions, the major requirement for mammalian survival in the ocean is heat retention.

Three "mechanisms" have evolved in whales to help them sustain body temperatures averaging 37.8 degrees C (100 F). The smaller species eat enormous amounts of food; a harbor porpoise can consume as much as 25% of its body weight each day. By contrast, the great whales eat approximately 10% of their weight daily. For an 86-metric ton (95 t) blue whale, this works out to "only" 8.8 metric tons (9.5 t) of krill, and for a 36.3-metric ton (40 t) humpback it may mean locating and consuming "only" 3.6 metric tons (4 t) of sand launce. These larger species benefit from a second adaptation: their body volume (bulk) is very large in relation to their surface area, so they lose body heat less rapidly than do smaller species. Finally, increased blood flow to the fins and tail is apparently important in liberating excess heat on occasions when that is necessary; in dolphins, fins may be 8.3 degrees C (16 F) warmer than the flanks.

Another physiological adaptation is seen in the kidneys, which are made up of clusters of small lobes, or reniculi, resembling bunches of grapes. Whale kidneys are large, about twice the size of those in terrestrial mammals of comparable size and weight, and produce large volumes of urine. Ocean-dwelling dolphins have approximately six times the number of reniculi as freshwater dolphins of the Ganges River.

Various theories have been developed to explain the workings of cetacean kidneys. As with most questions of cetacean physiology and behavior, the renal system is an area about which very little is known. Nevertheless, researchers have offered some educated guesses. Whales may need kidneys of gargantuan size because they take in large amounts of seawater while feeding (and drink at least small amounts). As with all marine vertebrates, the salt concentration in a whale's body is lower than that of the surrounding ocean; a whale's body tissues lose water due to a tendency to reach an equilibrium with the higher salt levels of the surrounding water. This is similar to the process that takes place when humans go swimming in saltwater and emerge with shriveled fingers and a strong thirst. In whales the situation is exacerbated by the large amounts of seawater taken in during feeding. To expel excess salts, it is probable that cetaceans pass a considerable amount of water through their kidneys. There is evidence that cetaceans do produce an abundance of urine of the same salinity as their blood, and that under some conditions they may produce concentrated urine. Either condition could explain the large kidneys.

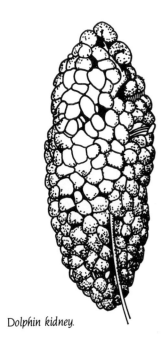

Dolphin kidney.

Breathing

Although whales appear fishlike and live in the ocean, the similarity is a superficial one. Whales are mammals with lungs and must come to the surface to breathe. If a whale is trapped or otherwise unable to reach the surface, it will drown. Whales employ 85% to 90% of their total lung capacity when inhaling, compared to the 15% used by humans. The lungs of a great whale can hold more than 2000 liters of air; human lungs have a capacity of about 4 liters when the body is in a state of exertion, but normal intake rarely exceeds 2 liters.

The cetacean nose, called a blowhole, is located at the top of the head. Toothed whales have a single external opening, and baleen whales have two, although all whales have a double nasal opening in the skull.

The great whales generally take a breath at 10-second to 2-minute intervals (one inhalation-exhalation cycle lasts 2 seconds or less). A very rough rule of thumb holds that they blow once for each minute spent submerged. After breathing on the surface for a period lasting from several seconds to several minutes, whales dive to feed, travel or rest. They generally remain submerged for 2-10 minutes, but they sometimes stay under for as long as 40 minutes. A submerged sperm whale may remain below the surface for over an hour and dive 1.5 km (1 mile) or more.

The "blow," or exhaled breath of whales, is a mixture of gases, water droplets and some mucous. When a whale submerges, a few seconds pass between the final inhalation and the shutting of the blowhole. Liters of water pour in through the nostrils, but muscles deeper inside the head close off the nasal passages and prevent the water from entering the lungs. During the dive, the whale essentially holds its breath, and the air in the lungs is compressed and heated by the body. When the whale surfaces and exhales, the air expelled from the lungs mixes with the water in the nasal passage as it moves toward the blowhole. The rapid expansion and cooling of the gases that follow release into the outside air often cause the moisture in the breath to condense into a cloud that is visible for some distance.

Design for watery living: a whale's blowhole breaks the surface before most of the rest of its body. (Jane Gibbs photo)

The shape and height of a blow are so distinctive that they can be used to make a tentative species identification from over 800 meters away (½ mi). For example, the blow of the humpback is low and bushy, generally 3 to 3.5 m (10-12 ft) high, and about 2.5 m (8 ft) across. The finback's blow is tall (up to 6 m or 20 ft) and narrow. The right whale's blow, owing to the distance between its nostrils, forms a distinct V pattern and may be 4.5 m (15 ft) high. The sperm whale's blowhole is located on the left side of its forehead and directs the blow forward and up at a 45-degree angle. The blow of the minke whale, smallest of the baleen whales, is rarely visible, probably because of low moisture content. The comparably sized orca whale, however, has a very obvious blow, which suggests that size alone is not a factor in the visibility of exhaled breath. (It should be noted that wind conditions can alter the appearance of any blow and affect the accuracy of distant identifications.)

Locomotion

The movement of whales through water is fundamentally different from the way fish and seals swim. Most fish propel themselves with a horizontal movement of the body and tail; hair seals use their hind flippers in a horizontal motion; and whale-eared seals use their fore flippers in an up-and-down motion.

Whales swim forward by moving their tail flukes vertically. The upward movement provides the propulsive force; the down stroke stabilizes the whale, preparing it for the next upward movement. The flippers are used exclusively for steering and stabilization. Dorsal fins, absent in right, bowhead, sperm, and beluga whales, are larger in the faster swimmers and probably serve as stabilizers.

Whale muscle structure provides great leverage and power in each stroke, especially in the smaller species. Power muscles, like those of the tail and back, are attached to the vertebrae; tendons are attached directly to spinal processes and to specialized "chevron" bones on the vertebrae at the tail that help increase leverage for propulsion.

Variations on these generalized mechanisms for movement produce different travel speeds among whale species. The thick-blubbered rights and bowheads would overheat and perish if forced to move quickly for any length of time; they rarely travel at speeds above 5 knots. (A knot measures both distance and the speed at which it is traveled; when a boat or a whale travels at 1 knot, it covers 1 nautical mile in an hour. A nautical mile is roughly 2 kilometers or 1.15 miles.) Humpback whales tend to cruise at a similar speed, 3-5 knots, but they can reach 8 to 12 knots. Sperm whales have been reported traveling at 12 knots, but their usual speed is between 8 and 10. Finback and sei whales can travel at 20 knots, and finbacks chase schools of fish at speeds approaching 25 knots, often leaving the water entirely while in hot pursuit. None of the great whales, however, can match the incredible speeds of the dolphins, which have been clocked in excess of 40 knots.

Diving

Whales generally will not dive deeper than their food sources. Under normal conditions, some baleen whales do not descend below 18 m (60 ft), even though they are capable of much deeper dives. Many prey species — herring, sand launce, squid, krill, and capelin — can be found 3 to 15 m (10-50 ft) below the surface. By contrast, sperm whales are bottom feeders that sometimes travel as far as 800 m (½ mi) below the surface in search of prey. Drowned sperm whales have been found tangled in communication cables at depths of over 900 m (3000 ft), and

Comparative Speeds of Some Cetacean Species

The lower "cruising" figures represent a range of speeds within which individuals of the species can comfortably travel over extended periods. The higher speeds come in short bursts during feeding or when fleeing from danger.

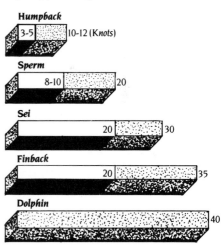

Humpback
3-5 10-12 (Knots)

Sperm
8-10 20

Sei
20 30

Finback
20 35

Dolphin
40

Humpback breaches, Gulf of Maine. (Jane Gibbs photo)

KUNST VOOR KRACHT.
VII.

Dutch engraving, 1657. (With the permission of the Folger Shakespeare Library)

sperm whale dives of 1.5 km (1 mi) straight down have been reported.

Significant physiological adaptations enable whales to dive for extended periods and to depths and pressures prohibitive to other mammals. In relation to body mass, the lung size and capacity of great whales is about one-half that of land mammals. Whales further reduce the chance of damage to their lungs and avoid possible buoyancy problems by exhaling before a deep dive. The smaller the amount of air in their lungs when they submerge, the greater the protection against lung damage.

When a whale blows on the surface, it accomplishes two things: waste elimination and hyperventilation. The blow replaces carbon dioxide in the bloodstream with oxygen. But rather than remaining in the blood as it does in humans, much of the oxygen binds chemically with red muscle pigment (myoglobin), giving the muscles a deep burgundy color distinctive to whales and seals. The blood is a transport medium as in humans, but the muscles retain increased amounts of oxygen, and only a small volume of gas actually remains in the lungs. Consequently, whales avoid "the bends" that afflict human divers with external air supplies who ascend rapidly from deep waters.

In effect, a whale becomes a heart-brain-kidney animal during its dives. Nonessential areas of the body — the flukes, flippers, and skin — are deprived of oxygen; only the major organs receive a supply. The heartbeat of the diving animal drops by 50% or more. In 1980, naturalists were able to monitor the heartbeat of a humpback whale trapped in Newfoundland's Trinity Bay. They found that a rate of 40 beats each minute at the surface dropped to 4 beats a minute when the whale submerged. (Similarly, rates of diving seals have been recorded dropping from 100 to 10 beats a minute.) Other body functions, like digestion, slow by 90% when the animal is below the surface, further conserving oxygen and energy.

This slowdown of bodily processes, called "bradychardia," is not the sole reason for the whales' diving abilities, nor is the affinity of their red muscle pigment for oxygen. An additional physiological adaptation helps to make their dives possible. Distributed throughout a whale's body are specialized areas of blood collection, the most important of which lies behind the thorax next to the backbone. Known as the *retia mirabilia* ("wondrous net"), these massive networks of small arteries and veins embedded in fat hold significant amounts of blood. The artery walls in the *retia mirabilia* are lined with muscle tissue, giving them the strength and flexibility to withstand quick changes of blood pressure and volume.

One final point about the remarkable diving abilities of whales may also relate to the presence of the *retia*. In addition to the ability of cetacean physiological processes to function at great depths and pressures, they function while the whale's body is being subjected to different levels of pressure. When a large whale sounds, or dives below the surface, its brain may be 18 m (60 ft) below its flukes. The body thus experiences from 1 to 3 atmospheres of pressure simultaneously (an atmosphere is the measure of air pressure normally encountered at sea level; underwater, pressure increases with depth at the rate of one atmosphere for each additional 10 meters or 33 feet). There is evidence that the *retia* play a key role in maintaining an adequate supply of blood to head, thorax, and abdomen when a cetacean's body is subjected to this drastic pressure differential.

Cetacean Senses

The five senses in the cetacea range from an extremely well developed sense of hearing to a virtually nonexistent sense of smell. As an example of adaptation to a new environment, the evolution of cetacean senses demonstrates a fascinating shift from the general pattern common to land animals, which is assumed to resemble that of the whales' terrestrial ancestors.

A sense of smell above water is of little use to whales; apparently, it has equally few advantages to life below the surface. Throughout the cetaceans there is a trend toward a reduction in olfactory structures. In the baleen whales only traces of the olfactory nerve and mucous membrane are evident, and in the toothed whales not even vestigial structures can be found.

The sense of touch in whales is poorly understood. There are many indications of whale skin sensitivity. Observers at close quarters report that the skin of a great whale shudders when it is touched. Humpback whales have been seen lying on their sides touching the hulls of wooden sailing vessels with their long flippers. Captive dolphins seem to delight in being petted and are seen rubbing themselves against the sides and bottoms of their tanks.

The sense of taste may be reasonably well-developed in some species. Dolphins, at least, show a preference for their favorite foods when choices are presented. Although the snouts of several species have many hairs, the function of these hairs is not clear. They may enable a whale to detect current direction or disturbances in the water.

Generally, sight is less important for cetaceans than for terrestrial mammals. Even in shallow areas, visibility in the ocean is often limited, and vision provides little help for navigation. Under certain circumstances, good eyesight at close range may have advantages. In the clear tropical waters where humpbacks mate and

The patterns on humpback flukes are as characteristic of an individual whale as fingerprints are of a human. Although whales probably rely heavily on sonic communication, vision may play a part in helping them identify other individual whales among a larger group. (Gleyn C. Noble photo, lower right/ all others Jane Gibbs)

calve, for example, close-range vision may help individual whales identify other whales by their distinctive flipper and fluke patterns.

Another major exception to this reduction of sight in cetaceans is found in dolphins. Observations of wild dolphins leaping over 6 m (20 ft) above the ocean surface suggest they are searching for distant flocks of birds whose position indicates the location of schools of fish. Groups of dolphins have been seen swimming toward large flocks of birds, apparently after spotting them from as far away as 8 km (5 mi). If this is the case, these animals not only can see small objects at impressive distances, but can focus instantly when leaving the water. Recent studies of the eyes of small cetaceans suggest that lens accommodation permits such visual acuity.

The vision of baleen whales is restricted in an additional way. Because their eyes are set far back and low on the sides of their heads, great whales have primarily lateral vision; only certain small cetaceans have forward binocular vision. Sometimes a whale will engage in "spy-hopping" and raise itself vertically above the water, the only position from which it can scan the surface.

Despite these limitations, several adaptations enhance vision and protect a whale's eyes. A shimmering membrane called the tapetum lies just behind the retina. It reflects light back into the retina, effectively doubling the amount of light the whale receives. Well-developed ocular rods also seem to magnify light levels. Oily secretions from the Harderian glands wash the eye's outermost layer, which itself is thicker and harder than the corresponding layer in land mammals. Both these adaptations protect the sensitive cornea and lens from injury as the cetacean swims through water.

Two orca whales spyhopping to scan the water's surface. (Ken Balcomb photo)

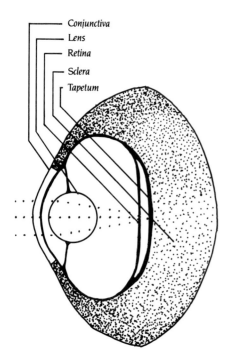

Conjunctiva
Lens
Retina
Sclera
Tapetum

The whale's eye reflects a number of adaptations that enhance vision in an aquatic environment. A thick enclosing sphere called the sclera maintains the eyeball's oval shape, which is important to proper focusing of images on the retina. Without it, the eyeball would become rounded under the great pressures encountered during dives. Light passing through the round lens is bent and produces a brighter image. The bending also helps correct for the refraction of light under water. The tapetum reflects light back onto the retina, effectively doubling the dim light that reaches the eye. Protection against injury comes from the thick conjunctiva and from glandular secretions that wash the eyeball's outermost layer.

In the twilight world of the whales, perceptions of the environment, of companions, enemies, and prey come from sound "pictures." The animals employ a sonarlike system called echolocation. It is well developed in the toothed whales; its functioning in the baleen whales remains uncertain, although these whales are known to emit far-reaching, low-pitched sounds.

Because seawater and flesh have essentially the same density, sound penetrates the flesh of submerged animals — people included — and stops when it hits the denser bones of the skull. Humans hear sound under water but cannot tell from what direction it comes. Whales have underwater directional hearing. A foamy mass around each inner ear guarantees its acoustic integrity and insulates it from the skull bone.

Cetaceans emit sound waves that travel until they reach an object of different density than the surrounding seawater. The waves bounce off the object and return to the sender. A toothed whale receives the sound, actually an echo, through its oil-filled lower jaw. The sound travels through a region called the "acoustic window" to the inner ear, where it is translated into nerve impulses that are relayed to the brain for processing. Echoes are also received by the "melon," the fatty organ perched on the whale's forehead that gives certain species a "thinker's brow" silhouette. The melon sends information along a similar path to the brain.

Once received in the brain, these signals provide a host of information about the object, including distance, direction, speed of movement, form, and density.

This system involves several specialized body structures unique to cetaceans. The acoustic window is a thin, hollow shell of bone located in the lower jaw just in front of the inner ear. Functionally, it works as part of the cetacean ear. The melon both receives echoes and beams sound. Although its ability to transmit is poorly understood, the melon can perform both of these functions simultaneously.

Cetaceans produce their characteristic high and low sounds by forcing air from the nasal passage into sacs and through valves. A crude approximation for humans involves taking in a mouthful of air, then closing the mouth, pinching the nostrils shut, and trying to force the air out through the blocked passages. The result is a series of barely audible pops and squeaks. In effect, this is the method employed by the cetacea, which have no vocal cords. Their respiratory systems include complicated arrangements of sacs for pushing air around in order to produce these sounds. The system is far more developed in the toothed whales than in the baleen whales.

The cetacean "voice" has a dual purpose. It is a tool of social communication that helps the mammal maintain contact with companions, and it serves as the navigational beacon used in echolocation. Dolphins can use both functions simultaneously. A dolphin's voice is made up of strings of clicks or pops that can be started or stopped instantaneously and directed with precision. Similarly, the receiver can tell exactly the source and location of the transmitter. Each cetacean species makes a distinctive sound that other species members can recognize, but communication may also occur between species.

Echolocation is possible because water is so dense, compressing rather than scattering sound and transmitting it five times faster than does air. These properties of water have prompted some cetologists to speculate that the great whales communicate across hundreds of miles using only the sounds produced within their bodies.

When echolocating, whales transmit up to 300 clicks a second, and can change their frequency in less than one thousandth of a second. The sounds may be short, high-pitched, and rapid, or long, low-pitched, and far apart. The higher frequencies are effective for close-range scanning, and the lower frequencies are used over longer distances. The clicks are apparently sent out in a sequence designed to avoid interference from incoming echoes, yet, even when the two overlap, cetaceans manage to extract information from the signals received.

Sperm whales, which spend considerable time in extremely deep and dark waters, survey their world with low, intense sounds. Among the baleen whales, blue whales and finbacks emit extremely low and intense sounds that probably have a communication function. Right whales have been recorded making extraordinarily complex noises. The gray whale also is quite vocal, a trait that may aid in navigation or communication.

The humpback, also known as the "singing" whale, vocalizes at its subequatorial breeding and calving grounds, although recordings have recently been made in its feeding grounds, too. The songs are composed of moans, yups, chirps, ooo's, who's, cries, snores, eeee's, and groans. All males in a given area sing the same song, and all are singing it when they arrive at the breeding grounds. How the singers learn the song is unknown, but the limited vocalizations heard on the summer feeding grounds may be "rehearsals." Possibly parts of the songs are created, practiced, and communicated to other whales during the migration between summer and winter grounds.

Thus far, all singing humpbacks have been identified as lone, unpaired males. A spatial distribution pattern makes it easier for single females to isolate a singer. The males spread themselves evenly over the banks according to their numbers, with large gaps when few callers are present and smaller spaces when the banks are crowded. They repeat the song over and over, presumably all winter if they find no mate but remain motivated to search for one. The songs are repetitious (but contain a sufficient variety of sounds so that human listeners do not find them unbearably monotonous). Presumably, a male who attracts a mate does not sing the next season if he remains mated. This reduces competition for young whales "coming of age."

The songs change slowly, but not completely; each new "arrangement" includes bits of previous songs, which indicates that the memories of humpbacks are well-developed. The redundancy of the songs suggests that they may contain specific information; the change in songs over the year may in some way aid the whales in keeping track of a year's passage, and may be of significance in herd recognition.

The humpback is the only species known to call in this way, and the origin of the singing is unclear. For whatever reason it began, calling probably now has a migratory function as well as reproductive and social significance.

Sexual Dimorphism

The bodies of most great whales do not exhibit dramatic gender-related differences. Among the baleen whales, the females generally attain greater proportions than the males. Female blues average 25 meters (81 feet), males generally about 23 m (76 ft). Similarly, female finbacks average 21 m (69 ft) and female humpbacks, 14.5 m (48 ft). Their male counterparts usually grow to about 19.5 m (64 ft) and 13.5 m (44 ft), respectively. The reverse is true with the toothed species, and the most striking example of size differences occurs with sperm whales. Males commonly reach a length of 15 m (50 ft) and a weight of 36.3 to 45 metric tons (40-50 t), and whaling ship records include reports of sperm whales as long as 21.3 m (70 ft). Female sperm whales never achieve these dimensions; they usually grow no larger than 11.5 m (38 ft) and 32 metric tons (35 t). Killer whales or orcas show similar size differentiation. Males may attain 9 m (30 ft) in length, whereas females may reach 7.5 m (25 ft). There are also significant differences in the development of body features among orcas. Perhaps the most striking example of dimorphism in orcas is the dorsal fin, which reaches a height of 2 m (6 ft) in males, compared to 1 m (3 ft) in females. Among the smaller toothed cetaceans, the dolphins and porpoises, gender-related differences in body size are insignificant.

Age Determination

It is believed that great whales live for 60 to 90 years, but none of the methods yet devised for determining age is completely reliable. Most of these estimation techniques determine relative, not precise, age.

** *Baleen*: Ridges on the plates of baleen whales correspond to periods of growth. These in turn represent periods of active feeding, which alternate with periods of fasting during migrations or shortages of food. By counting the growth periods, the minimum age of a whale can be estimated.

** *Ovaries*: The ovaries of mature females show a scar for each ovulation. If the age of sexual maturity of a particular species is known, that number plus the number of scars gives an approximate age for that female whale.

** *Ear Plugs*: Ear plugs are long structures of successive layers inside the ear canals of baleen whales. Until recently, scientists thought that each layer represented one year. However, wide discrepencies have been found between age estimates based on plugs taken from some tagged whales and the probable age of the whales based on their tagging dates. In some cases, apparently, two layers are produced each year.

** *Teeth*: A horizontal slice through a whale's tooth reveals distinct layers resembling the age rings in the trunk of a felled tree. It is possible that a whale's absolute age can be determined by counting these growth layers.

Like every other aspect of the cetacean life cycle, aging remains something of a mystery to researchers because there are so few chances to observe the animals in their accustomed habitats. Nevertheless, fairly reliable records suggest some likely lifespans for a number of species:

blue whale . . . . .95 years
finback whale . . . . .95 years
sperm whale . . . . .75 years
sei whale . . . . .70 years
orca whale . . . . .40 years
Dolphins and porpoises usually reach 25-30 years of age.

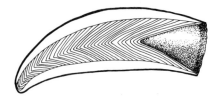

Two methods commonly used to estimate the age of whales: A slice down the vertical axis of a tooth (above) reveals a chevron pattern, each layer of which is thought to represent a year of age. The method is obviously restricted to **odontoceti,** *which include the sperm and orca whales, dol-*

phins and porpoises. Examination of a female whale's ovaries can usually provide enough information to estimate her age with some accuracy (right). Females ovulate only once each year, and if an egg is not fertilized, the **corpus luteum** *that forms during the cycle will waste away. Although it eventually shrinks to a ball with a diameter of 1-2 cm (1 in), it remains in the ovary for the life of the whale. By adding the total of these bodies, called* **corpora albicantia,** *in a given whale's ovary to the average age of sexual maturity for that species, scientists can estimate the female's age with some assurance.*

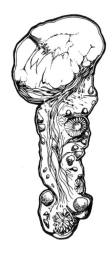

Intelligence and Behavior

Intelligence

The question of cetacean intelligence sparks considerable discussion among scientists and nonscientists. The idea that whales have mental processes equal or superior to those of human beings explains in part the public outcry over whaling.

Despite this sentiment, humans have not discovered a way to measure the intelligence of another species directly. Observations of daily problem-solving by animals and of relationships within and between species are intriguing. They inevitably tempt people to examine the animals in question through the special prism used to view human mental abilities that we call intelligence. Ultimately, such efforts become entangled in human subjectivity, and the process of determining animal intelligence becomes as unscientific as judging which animals are most valuable, most repulsive, or most endearing.

Whales have been central to this puzzle for years. The difficulty of trying to gauge the intelligence of nonhumans without even the crudest comparative yardstick is almost insurmountable. The fact that humans are rarely able to observe great whales over long periods of time only complicates the problem. To what do we compare them? The enduring cockroach? The highly manipulative chimp? The exceptional human like Emily Dickinson or Albert Einstein? Comparisons simply are not feasible. Because cetaceans lack hands — a feature humans consider important because it enables them to alter the physical environment — cetaceans are considered nonmanipulative problem-solvers. Beyond the assumption such a label makes about the *value* of this particular skill, the judgment may in fact be premature. The varied tactics of the bubble feeding strategy employed by humpback whales may be as ingenious as the human idea of beating a bush to flush out game or bending a leaf to cup drinking water.

Much has been made of brain-size-to-body-size ratio as a measure of intelligence. In fact, if brain size alone were the criterion, dolphins would easily be equal to, if not brighter than, humans. In strict physiological terms, a more useful consideration is the level of development in areas of the brain that control critical functions and the development of the cetacean neocortex or "new brain area."

The brain of every animal is divided into hemispheres, which are subdivided into lobes. Human brains have three lobes in each hemisphere, cetaceans have four. In human brains, the sensory and motor functions are contained in the third lobe. This is presumed to be the case with cetaceans, but the function of the fourth lobe is poorly understood. It may simply be a continuation of those motor and sensory areas. The neocortex is the "new" part of the brain. It is a cellular layer that covers each lobe and is not found in the ancestral condition. The lobes of the cetacean brain that would receive sensory images are well developed, enlarged, and highly convoluted. In animals, convolution is generally considered an indicator of the complexity of brain functions.

The form of cetacean brains reflects the requirements of the physical environment in which they evolved. Life in the ocean demands different sensing abilities from a mammal than does life on land. Of the five senses, hearing and sight become the primary modes of sensory reception in water, with hearing far more advanced because sound travels better underwater. In the absence of hands and fingers important to sensing on land, the head of the cetacean becomes the most important receptor of sensory data.

Conservationist Joan McIntyre has argued that human study of cetacean mental

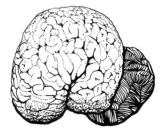

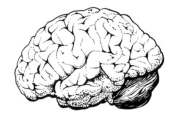

Relative brain sizes for dolphins (above) and humans. Dolphins compare favorably with humans in characteristics that humans associate with intelligence, such as brain-to-body-size ratio and density of brain lobe convolutions. Whether this proves the intellectual equality of the two species (or the superiority of the dolphin) has not been established — at least, not as far as humans are concerned.

processes is flawed by the assumption that intelligence *per se* ought to be the focus of that research. She suggests that *awareness*, a quality humans have long ascribed to themselves alone, should be the focus of attention. Yet, reports of dozens of human encounters with whales and dolphins "show a very specific awareness" on the part of cetaceans: an "awareness of the event, the exact placement of each individual in the event, an awareness of consequence, and a clear intent." McIntyre argues that this is a far more fruitful area for exploration than searching for signs of intelligence as we understand it.

No matter what formulation we adopt, it will very likely be some time before the intelligence question is understood, let alone solved. If some of the pioneer researchers in the field of cetacean intelligence and communication are correct, however, we may receive the answer directly from the animals themselves.

Feeding

Feeding patterns of whales are as specialized as the animals themselves. Maintaining such bulk requires massive supplies of food and highly evolved systems for catching and digesting it. As whales increased in size during the course of their evolution, teeth could not provide the amounts of food certain groups of them needed to survive. Of the great whales, only the sperm whale has teeth; other toothed whales are generally smaller in size.

Teeth were replaced in the other great whales by a filtering device made up of baleen. Baleen consists of long, narrow plates that hang from the whale's upper jaw where most other mammals would have teeth. Depending on the species, there can be as few as 160 plates on each side of the jaw (gray whale) to over 360 on a side (in the blue whale). The plates are made of keratin, the same material as in human fingernails, and they grow throughout the whale's life. The inside edge of each plate is covered with a fine fringe that adds significantly to its filtering qualities. Baleen shapes and sizes are distinctive for different species of whales. Gray whales, for example, have short baleen (20 cm/8 in) that is coarse and tough; right whale baleen measures 2.1 m (7 ft) in length, and a bowhead's baleen can be as long as 4 m (14 ft). Until the late 19th century, the flexibility of baleen plates made them important to the manufacture of such products as corset stays, umbrella ribs, riding whip handles, and even bedsprings.

In the rorqual whales — which include humpback, finback, Minke, blue, Bryde's and sei whales — the baleen is accompanied by an expandable throat and chest area. Numerous pleats in the flesh of the whale, extending from its chin to its belly, allow this area to expand. (Depending on the species, there may be as few as 30 or as many as 100; in addition, gray whales have a small number of shorter pleats.) These pleats accommodate the huge mouthfuls of water a rorqual whale takes in and passes through its relatively short baleen plates when it is feeding. Right and bowhead whales, which are nonrorquals, do not engulf their food this way. Instead, they "graze" by swimming slowly and evenly through the water.

Baleen whales can be distinguished by their feeding strategies: the *skimmers*, or right and bowhead whales; the *lungers*, the rorqual group of Minke, humpback, finback, blue, Bryde's, and sei whales; and the *bottom feeders*, or gray whales. In recent years sei whales have been observed skimming plankton, an uncharacteristic feeding method which suggests that they are broadening their ecological niche in response to the declining population of right whales. Since the right whales now consume a significantly smaller proportion of plankton, the seis may be adding this suddenly plentiful food to their diets.

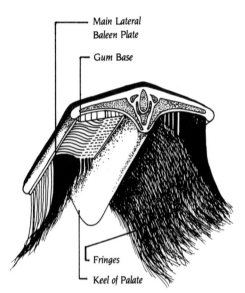

Main Lateral
Baleen Plate

Gum Base

Fringes

Keel of Palate

View from inside a baleen whale's mouth. The outer edge of each baleen plate is smooth, but the inner edge ends in a fine, hairy fringe. In both rorqual and nonrorqual baleen whales, this fringe prevents the escape of prey species — krill, copepods and certain kinds of fish — once they have entered the mouth. The nonrorqual right and bowhead whales "graze" in areas of heavy planktonic concentration. Moving slowly through the ocean, they allow water and swarms of krill to enter their mouths at the front. The water continues out the back, but the organisms are trapped on the hairy fringe. The nonrorquals periodically clean the fringe with their tongues, swallow, and recommence feeding.

Baleen drying in San Francisco, 1870s. With the completion of a transcontinental railroad in 1869, American whaleship owners found they could base their fleets on the Pacific coast and still serve the large eastern market. Prices for whale oil sagged after the Civil War, but demand for baleen remained high. Toward the end of the century, the discrepancy between the market values of these two commodities grew so great that California whaling crews working in the Arctic frequently cut out the jaws of dead whales, then set the carcasses adrift without bothering to strip them of blubber. (The Whaling Museum, New Bedford, Mass.)

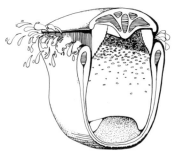

The feeding sequence for all rorquals appears to be similar. Before feeding, a whale's mouth is closed (view from inside, top). The mouth opens for feeding as the whale plunges into a concentration of fish or plankton, and the pleated skin on its throat unfolds to take in large volumes of water (middle). With its mouth full, the whale closes its jaw until only the baleen is exposed, then begins to contract its throat pleats and force water out through the baleen (bottom). As with the nonrorquals, the fringe traps fish and small organisms, which the whale licks off with its tongue.

A rorqual whale approaches its quarry at up to 30 km (20 mi) an hour, occasionally rising completely out of the water while in pursuit. Rolling onto one side, the whale opens its mouth (which may span 6 m(20 ft) in the larger species) and plows into its intended target, usually a school of fish or planktonic crustaceans called krill. As it hits the school, the weight of the load taken into its mouth may exceed 27 metric tons (30 t), depending on the size of the whale. The pleats expand the throat to enormous proportions. After securing the mouthful the whale closes its jaws until just the baleen is exposed. The animal then contracts the muscles that run the length of the pleats. This sudden constriction of the throat, combined with expulsive tongue motion, forces the water out through the sieve-like baleen. The plankton and fish that are the whale's food are caught by the fine plates of the baleen. The whale swallows this mouthful, then prepares to lunge again, repeating the process until its appetite is satisfied.

Right and bowhead whales filter minute planktonic organisms from the surface waters while swimming at a slow, steady pace through the plankton cloud. Water flows in, around, and out through the long plates of the baleen. The whales lick the plankton from the plates with their tongues before swallowing, often making a smacking sound in the process.

California gray whales "plow" along the ocean bottom while turned to one side with their mouths open. Analysis of the contents from gray whale stomachs consistently reveals high concentrations of bottom-dwelling organisms. Amounts of silt, mud, and sand, and bits of kelp have also been recovered. A gray's sturdy, thick baleen is crucial to this feeding pattern.

Toothed sperm whales are another bottom-feeding species. Sperm whale carcasses found tangled in deep submarine cables are thought to be victims of their feeding habits. It is theorized that while plowing the soft ocean bottom for squid or other food at depths where there is practically no light, the whales snag their lower jaws on the cable. As they struggle to break free, they further entangle themselves and eventually drown.

Sperm whales apparently employ two other methods to obtain food. They may rely on echolocation to beam in on their prey, which is otherwise invisible in the dark sea. In addition, they are believed capable of setting a special kind of trap for various large species of squid. As a whale lies motionless above the ocean floor, phosphorescent phytoplankton that live in its mouth emit a faint glow. In the blackness that prevails at these depths, the light attracts nearby squid, and when one swims close enough, the whale snaps its jaws shut and swallows its prey.

Whales swallow their food whole. The food enters the first of three specialized cetacean stomachs, a holding sac for material arriving from the esophagus. This stomach functions as a gizzard similar to that of birds, crushing the food with strong muscular action. From the gizzard, food travels through a narrow tube to the main stomach, where it is further broken down by digestive acids. The third, or pyrolic stomach, receives this material from the main stomach. It separates the nutrients, which are absorbed into the blood stream, and allows wastes to continue through the intestine. With one exception, the cetacean intestinal tract is relatively short, with virtually no distinction between the large and small intestines. Sperm whales, however, have intestines that reach 160 meters (525 ft).

A humpback feeding off the coast of New Hampshire. The pleats have allowed the throat to expand to several times its original volume. When the whale closes its mouth, the water will be forced through the short baleen plates visible on the upper jaw, trapping fish and plankton for the whale to swallow. Occasionally, a miscalculating gull ends up as part of a humpback's meal. This one escaped. (Jane Gibbs photo)

Breeding

Great whales generally mate and calve in warm waters during the winter. There are exceptions to this pattern, and the habits of a few species are completely unknown.

Mating behavior begins with a long session of attentive, physical, and very tender foreplay. Both partners roll together, rubbing and patting one another with flippers and flukes. Copulation takes place with the partners belly to belly, lined up horizontally or vertically. The penis extends from the body wall of the male through the genital slit located just behind the umbilicus. This is the only time it ever extrudes from the body. The testicles, permanently tucked into the body, lie behind the kidneys. The female sex organs include the vagina, a mucous membrane, a uterus, Fallopian tubes, and ovaries that are located behind the kidneys in the same spot as the male testicles. Each yearly ovulation produces a permanent growth on the ovaries that is useful to researchers in making reliable estimates of age. Although whales undergo an annual estrus, they may be sexually active at various times of the year; however, cows seldom produce offspring every year.

After mating, the female carries the developing fetus for 10-12 months. During the summer, she feeds extensively on plankton and fish, fattening herself and nourishing the unborn calf. Once back in the tropical water of the winter breeding areas, she delivers a single calf (or sometimes twins, which occur with about the same frequency as in humans). The calf nurses for 6 to 14 months, depending on species, after which it begins taking its own food.

The calf is born tail first, the inverse of human babies, after an unknown period of labor. As a rough comparison, dolphins in aquaria endure labors lasting 90 to 120 minutes. Delivery can only be described as monumental: a sperm whale calf measures about 3.6 meters (12 ft) and weighs 970 kilograms (2600 pounds); a finback calf, about 5.5 m (18 ft) and 1350 kg (3600 lb); and blue whale calves, up to 6.5 m (21 ft) and 1500 kg (4000 lb). After delivering the calf, the mother nudges the newborn to the surface for its first breath of air.

The nipples of the mother are enclosed in the body wall. Whales lack true lips, so the calf pushes its mouth against the slit, and the milk is sprayed into its throat by powerful muscles that surround the nipple. This is done quickly, as calves must surface for air more often than adults.

The milk is 40% to 50% butterfat (compared to 4% in cow's milk), low in sugar, and high in calcium and phosphorus; its protein content is double that of human milk. This formula enables the calf to survive in its new environment, largely by helping it grow quickly, since it has no hair and cannot nestle against its mother for warmth like other newborn mammals. Its body rapidly converts the milk's butterfat into blubber, and the extra calcium and phosphorus encourage rapid growth of bones. In the first seven months outside the womb, for example, a blue whale calf can grow more than 7.5 m (25 ft) and gain over 22.5 metric tons (25 t).

In many species, an adult male acts as an escort for the nursing mother and calf. The escort may release noisy blasts of air to distract an intruder, or he will place his body between the calf and danger. Adult humpback whales have been seen nudging curious calves away from boats with humans aboard. If confronted by sharks, the two adults will sandwich the calf between them. Presumably the same behavior is initiated if the group feels threatened by orcas, which are known to attack feeble adults and calves of many species of large whales.

Birth of a cetacean: An orca delivery at Marineland, California, in late 1978. Cetacean calves emerge from the womb tail first, a reversal of the pattern in humans. (Marineland photo)

Sleep

The process of sleep in whales, as in all animals, is a subject of great interest to human investigators. Because whales are ocean dwellers, they have special sleeping requirements. They cannot simply drop off into a deep sleep, or they will sink below the surface and drown.

Very little is known of the pattern of sleep in cetaceans. Researchers speculate that a part of the brain "shuts down" for a short duration in a kind of catnap. On awakening, the rested part of the brain assumes the task of maintaining bodily functions, and the previously active section takes its turn resting. John Lilly, a pioneer researcher in the field of dolphin biology, found that captive dolphins shut first one eye then the other for 10 to 15 minutes at a time. He estimated that in a 24-hour period, each eye was closed for a total of 3 to 4 hours. During this time, the dolphins continued to move slowly around their tank.

Baleen whales rest on the surface for undetermined periods of time. Observations of resting whales reveal a rhythmic pattern consisting of four or five exhalations spaced three minutes apart, then submergence. After four or five minutes under water they "bob" up in the same spot, releasing an explosive blow as they do. While asleep, their blows have a loud "snoring" quality. They repeat this process several times, then apparently "wake up" and move off slowly.

Nocturnal Behavior

Observations of whale behavior at night are understandably rare; however, researchers and fishermen report much activity after dark. Behaviors identified both by sound and available moonlight include feeding, breaching, and flipper slapping — in short, nearly every action observed during daylight.

Ecology

The marine ecosystem is a complex and fragile tapestry of interwoven biological, physical, and chemical threads. The disappearance of any one strand may not destroy the fabric, but it weakens the cloth slightly and leaves the adjoining threads more vulnerable to damage. In nature, the loss of any one species, worldwide or regionally, causes degradation, stress, and readjustments within the ecosystem.

Food chains are networks of interdependent living organisms. Energy and nutrients pass up the chains, creating and sustaining life. Food webs link numerous food chains and represent an added order of complexity. The loss of any one link weakens the structure of the food chain and adds to existing environmental stresses on the organisms that relied upon the lost member. Further losses may cause the entire scheme to collapse.

Sunlight is the primary source of energy for life on earth. Green plants use it to combine carbon dioxide and water into carbohydrates, the energy form which organisms use to produce other organic compounds. Oxygen is released into the atmosphere as a by-product of this process. Surface waters of the ocean are layered with minute green plants called phytoplankton that serve as food for tiny animal plankton called zooplankton. Small fish species feed on the zooplankton, which drift with ocean currents in vast marine pastures. Larger fish — mackerel, bluefish and some squid species — feed on the small fish, and even larger fish, such as tuna, feed on these species. Whales enter the chain at several levels. They may feed on krill and other zooplankton, squid, or fish; orcas feed directly on tuna, as well as on smaller species of fish and other marine mammals. The diversity of more complex food webs helps to create more stable environments. This simplified description only suggests the structure and complexity of a marine food chain, since in life thousands of species are involved, each interconnected to others in varying degrees.

The possible effects of the loss of great whales on the ocean's food chains and webs are uncertain. Whales enter food chains and webs at many levels, and, like any important consumer, help to check the populations of their prey species. Since the depletion of many great whale stocks in the Arctic, for example, the krill population has mushroomed. The ageless balance has been tipped, and adjustments throughout the system are necessary to establish a new equilibrium.

Human Relations with Whales

Beginnings

We do not know when humans first showed interest in whales, but a handful of artifacts survives to tantalize us with hints. Animal bone harpoons much bigger than anything needed to capture fish have been found throughout the Basque country of northwestern Spain and southwestern France. The Basques were known as industrious whalers during the Middle Ages, but these harpoons suggest that their ancestors pursued the hunt as early as 16,000 BC. In the islands north of the Scottish coast, stone cutting blades from several prehistoric sites have been identified as blades for "flensing," or stripping the blubber from a whale's carcass. Caves in Norway have yielded detailed drawings and carvings of whales, some of which may date back to 8000 BC, and all of which are at least 4,000 years old. On Sakhalin Island north of Japan, archeologists have unearthed bone tools incised with the unmistakable images of whales and whaling crews. They date from between 4000 and 2000 BC and are the earliest representations of the actual whaling process yet identified. In Alaska, excavations of Eskimo middens (kitchen trash heaps) have yielded whale bones deposited around 1400 BC.

By the time of the Sakhalin and Alaskan artifacts, humans had begun to leave records of their activities, and we can turn to rich oral and written history for a finer sense of human attitudes toward whales. Creation legends from the cultures of Oceania describe Vatea, the father of the human race, as "half man and half fish, the division being like the two halves of the human body. The species of fish to which this great divinity was allied being the taairangi (cetacea), or great sea monsters...."

In western cultures, the whale is among the first animals mentioned in the Old Testament of the Judeo-Christian Bible (Genesis 1:21), and it appears again in the Book of Job (41):

I will not conceal his parts, nor his power, nor his
   comely proportion....
He maketh the deep to boil like a pot;
he maketh the sea like a pot of ointment.
He maketh a path to shine after him;
one would think the deep to be hoary.
Upon the earth there is not his like, who
is made without fear.
He beholdeth all high things:
he is king over all the children of pride.

From the Book of Psalms (104: 25-26) comes this passage:

So is this great and wide sea, wherein are things creeping innumerable, both small and great beasts. There go the ships, there is that Leviathan, whom hast made to play therein.

The sense of awe is scarcely hidden in these biblical passages dedicated to whales. There is no mention of the kill or economics; these early interpreters ranked the whale among the world's wondrous creations and mystifying occurrences.

This 3,500-year-old frieze from Crete may be the earliest picture of dolphins created by a human — which makes the anatomical accuracy of its subjects even more remarkable. The dolphins were painted on the walls of the Queen's Megaron in the Royal Palace at Knossos sometime between 2000 and 1500 BC. (University of New Hampshire photo)

(left) An interpretation of the story of Jonah from the **Amesbury Psalter,** an illuminated English manuscript completed in the years before 1255. The "great fish" that swallows Jonah is generally assumed to have been a whale. At least one modern case of survival in a whale's stomach (1891) has been documented.

In the Book of Jonah (1:17) a whale rescues Jonah after he has been cast from a boat into rough seas: "Now the Lord had prepared a great fish to swallow up Jonah, and Jonah was in the belly of the fish for three days and three nights." The "great fish," a whale, becomes in this passage the vehicle of divine mercy.

Cetaceans appear in writings and art left by other branches of western culture. In 1100 BC, Assyrian armies swept westward out of Mesopotamia to conquer the eastern shore of the Mediterranean. Whaling was unknown to this riverside people, and accounts of these conquests describe the amazement of King Tiglath-Pileser I on his discovery of the whaling activities he encountered in the Phoenician harbor towns of the region. "(I)n the ships of Arvad he rode," we learn from an obelisk commemorating the campaign, "a blower in the great sea he slew." Later Assyrian records show that the Phoenicians paid tribute to the empire partly in whale's teeth, a form of ivory highly prized among civilizations of the period.

Greek coins and jewelry from 500 BC bear images of dolphins, often shown accompanying humans. Paralleling the Jonah story, art work from this era and later periods frequently depicts humans being saved from drowning by dolphins. These are among the earliest such reports, and they have been validated by modern observation.

Around 350 BC the Greek philosopher and scientist Aristotle correctly classified cetaceans with mammals, not fish, in *History of the Animals*. He based his classification on four grounds. First, he pointed out, "Dolphins and whales and all such Cetacea have no gills, but they have a blowhole because they have a lung." Like more familiar land animals, he noted, their offspring develop from embryos,

Boy riding a dolphin. Detail from a floor mosaic in a Roman house at Delos, Greece.

not eggs; they give birth to live young; and they nurse their young on milk produced in their own bodies.

Four hundred years after Aristotle, Pliny the Elder criss-crossed the Mediterranean in the course of his career as a Roman administrator and military officer. An industrious amateur scholar, he produced a torrent of writings on a wide range of subjects, including natural science. Although he was not thorough as a naturalist, depending heavily on hearsay and previously published reports (some unreliable), his *Naturalis historia* was widely read. For centuries after his death in 79 AD he influenced the study of animals, much to the detriment of knowledge.

Pliny wrote about cetacea in *Naturalis historia*. Like Aristotle, he understood that dolphins breathe air, yet he steadfastly refused to believe that whales do the same. In fact, he could see no relation between the two. "The dolphin," he wrote, "is an animal that is not only friendly to mankind but is also a lover of music, and it can be charmed by singing in harmony. . . . It is not afraid of a human, but comes to meet vessels at sea and sports and gambols round them, actually trying to race them and passing them even when the vessels are under full sail." The larger whales, "armed with the most terrible sharpe and cutting teeth," were a different story. He described the "great hole in the forehead" of baleen whales, out of which gusted "mighty breath . . . like storms of rain," but he rejected the idea that they breathed with lungs as mammals do.

Pliny clearly favored the cheerful dolphins and was especially impressed with their speed, which he thought surpassed that of any land animal. He also claimed that dolphins, driven by a need for air after chasing fish underwater for long

Pliny reported that whales could swamp a ship with their spoutings, and for 1500 years the notion was widely accepted in Europe. In this woodcut from the early 16th century, the ship's cannons are useless against an enormous whale.

Dionysus escorted by dolphins on the Dionysus Cup, created by the artist Exekia about 540 BC.

We have some idea of the esteem the Greeks felt for dolphins from their close association with the gods in Greek mythology. Dolphins commonly travel with Poseidon and carry Aphrodite over the water in a seashell chariot. Eros is sometimes shown riding a dolphin. Dolphins also figure prominently in tales relating to Apollo's establishment of the oracle at Delphi. On this early Greek cup they accompany Thetis, one of Poseidon's attendants and mother of Achilles. (University of New Hampshire photo)

distances, could "shoot up like arrows from a bow in order to breathe again, and leap out of the water with such force that they often fly over a ship's sails." The ungainly whales, on the other hand, were simply "mighty masses and lumps of flesh without fashion." Pliny reported that the sperm whale "rears up like a vast pillar higher than a ship's rigging and belches out a sort of deluge of water."

Whether Pliny actually ever observed great whales at sea and was traumatized by the experience, or simply recounted stories of hysterical, possibly drunken sailors, is not clear. As mentioned, he relied heavily on reports written by earlier observers, some of them reliable, some not. In any case, it is difficult to relate his fear and hatred to more modern experience. Films and personal accounts of whales approaching small vessels and allowing themselves to be petted hardly fit the bloodthirsty image Pliny presented.

The dissimilar appearances and temperaments of dolphins and whales clearly fed prejudices, not only among Pliny's contemporaries, but for centuries to follow. Ships were small, the men that manned them even smaller, and a long ocean voyage bred boredom, homesickness, and fear. Under these circumstances, the sudden appearance of an 18-m (60-ft), foam-spouting creature which headed directly for the boat, then sounded and disappeared was an understandable cause for panic and the embroidered tales that inevitably followed. By comparison, the appearance of a school of 3-meter (10-foot) dolphins — grinning, racing, and leaping gleefully about the boat — was sheer entertainment.

Pliny included a half dozen stories about the special qualities of dolphins in *Naturalis historia*. He described instances of dolphins helping fishermen, playing with seaside bathers, and working together to rescue other dolphins trapped by humans. Many of his tales involve a special relationship between a boy and a dolphin. He cited six cases from various parts of the Mediterranean world, all similar to this one from the Gulf of Lucrinus.

A boy living in a coastal village frequently brought food to a dolphin that swam in the harbor. He befriended it to the point that the dolphin would come at his call, and for years the boy rode the dolphin to and from school in a neighboring village. They became so close, in fact, that some versions of the tale imply a sexual attraction between the two. When the boy became sick, then died, the mourning dolphin continued to wait at their customary meeting place. Eventually "for verie grief and sorrow" it died, too. In other tales of boy-dolphin love, the boy dies when he is accidentally impaled on the dolphin's sharp dorsal fin. In a dramatic display of its grief, the dolphin assures its own death by intentionally stranding itself on a nearby shore.

On the famous Dionysus Cup produced in Greece about 540 BC, seven dolphins escort a bejeweled man sailing a dolphin-shaped craft. The scene illustrates the story that Greek culture had accepted as an explanation of the animals' creation. While in human form Dionysus, the god of wine and pleasure, was captured by pirates. Convinced he was a prince, they planned to hold him for ransom. Unable to talk them out of their plan, Dionysus resorted to his supernatural powers. He transformed himself into different animals, including a lion and a bear, and caused grape vines to grow out of the ship's mast. The terrified crew members abandoned all thoughts of kidnapping and ransom and scrambled overboard. Poseidon, god of the sea, mercifully rescued them by transforming them into dolphins who retained human emotions and intellect. In gratitude they became the god's servants, obeying his commands and pulling his vessel through the seas. A Greek coin from the same era shows one of the dolphins rescuing Poseidon's son Tara from drowning. The Dionysus myth helped the ancient Greeks explain the dolphin's

cheerfulness, intelligence, and apparent love of people.

With a theme similar to that of the Dionysus/Poseidon myth, Herodotus related the tale of Arion, a popular musician who supported himself by giving concerts in Rome and the provinces. He played the harp so beautifully that his music was thought to be capable of dispelling the most violent impulses of human or beast. Following a particularly profitable series of recitals, the musician booked passage on a Corinthian vessel. Unfortunately, it was manned by a crew of pirates who were aware of his identity and wealth. They conspired to rob Arion and throw him overboard, and the musician was unable to discourage them. He finally talked them into letting him play his harp one last time before being forced overboard. His playing and singing, lovelier than ever before, failed to move the pirates but attracted dolphins to the ship's side. When Arion jumped into the water, one of them carried him safely to shore.

These myths convey several themes, which may be the basis for the contemporary popularity of cetaceans. In the Dionysus myth, evil men are transformed into good dolphins, and the dolphin thus symbolizes redemption. In the Jonah, Tara, and Arion myths, a cetacean rescues a good person from evil, and thus, symbolizes compassion, salvation, and justice. In all myths, dolphins represent the merciful side of the deep and dangerous ocean.

Delphinid fan club: Arion is rescued by dolphins attracted to the ship by his playing. The 17th-century engraver who created this scene had only the loosest notion of dolphin anatomy and gave the animals extra fins, bulging eyes, and the tailfins and scales of fish.

33

Ancient Whaling

For thousands of years, the discovery of a stranded whale must have been cause for great joy and celebration among coastal-dwelling peoples all over the globe. The flesh of the animal provided food for many days; the oil-rich blubber could be burned for light and heat; and the teeth, bones, and innards were valuable for tools, weapons, ornamentation, and construction of buildings and furniture. Eskimos, for example, used long baleen plates for sled runners.

Not all cultures waited for luck and nature to bring them whales; some groups actively stalked them. The Eskimos hunted several species of whales, including the great bowhead, from small, skin-covered boats called umiaks. Approaching the whale as quietly as possibly, they struck the animal with a harpoon tied to a rope made of animal tendons. An inflated animal bladder served as a float that would enable the hunters to track it. When the float surfaced, the hunters raced to the spot knowing that the wounded whale was just below and rising for air. As it emerged, more harpoons were thrown into it, eventually killing the animal.

In the Aleutian Islands, whale hunters preferred poison-tipped spears to ropes and floats, a method that subjected the whale to a particularly agonizing death. After striking their target, the Aleuts retreated to the shore and waited for the whale to die. Depending on its size, the process may have taken up to two days, and then the hunters could not be certain that the carcass would float. Since right and bowhead whales floated after death, they were preferred quarry, but no whale was rejected on the grounds of inconvenience.

Sperm whale stranded in the Netherlands, 1610. Such strandings were the subject of numerous engravings and prints in the 17th and 18th centuries, a period of explosive growth in commercial whaling throughout northern Europe.
(By permission of the Folger Shakespeare Library).

The poison these hunters used was produced from monkshood or alconite, plants common to the Aleutian and Pribilof Islands. The source of the poison was a jealously guarded secret among the close-knit hunters. Centuries later, the hunters devised imaginative "recipes" to satisfy bothersome, naive European and American explorers. For example, in an 1872 journal the French ethnographer Pinart dismissed one potion as impractical because it required "human grease, which has been prepared from the corpses of rich people whom the whalers have exhumed and put to boil."

Model of a umiak, the 10-m (30-ft) skin-covered boat traditionally used by Eskimos for hunting whales. (Smithsonian Institution photo)

Migratory coastal species, including bowheads, humpbacks, and gray whales, were hunted the length of North America's Pacific coast. Indigenous crews set out in 9- to 12-meter (30- to 40-foot) canoes armed with shell-tipped lances and harpoons and ropes fashioned from twisted bark. Each canoe often had its own harpoon design. After the first harpoon was sunk, the hunt was completed with much whooping and shouting because the hunters believed that the commotion further confused the terrified whale, hindering its escape. Once the whale was killed and beached, it was rationed according to the number of harpoons from each crew that were recovered from the carcass.

On the eastern coast of North America, indigenous peoples hunted some of the smaller whale species from canoes. Before the 16th century, large populations of whales lived off New England and the Canadian Maritimes, and strandings appear to have been common.

In Scandinavia, particularly in Norway, dolphins and smaller coastal whales were hunted for thousands of years. Crews of fishermen from coastal settlements would follow schools of whales as they swam into the fjords in pursuit of fish. Forming a line of boats which they augmented with nets, they would attempt to "stampede" the whales toward the shore at the narrow end of the inlet.

Whales played an important role in these simple societies. They were so highly valued as sources of food and raw materials that many of the aboriginal peoples of the northern Pacific petitioned their gods, through various rituals, to assure the annual migration of whales. They nevertheless accepted whales as the spiritual equals of humans and all other life. Some groups even offered prayers for the spirits of whales they had killed, and Eskimo whalers observed a ceremony honoring the continuity of life in which they threw whale skulls back into the sea so that the animals' spirits would live on.

Even acknowledging the wastefulness of some hunting methods, the scale and simple technological methods of these aboriginal whale hunts assured that they would have little affect on the populations of any species. It was the discovery of large numbers of whales by sailors and adventurers from nations with more complex technologies and different attitudes toward the animals themselves that led to the construction of large whaling fleets and the eventual exhaustion of whale stocks.

De Tritonibus. Lib.IV.   IOOI
PAN VEL SATYRVS MARINVS.

Iconem hanc ichthyocentauri, siue dæmonis marini, vt ita dicam, à pictore quodam olim accepi:
qui talis monstri sceleton Antuerpiæ depictum se accepisse aiebat. Alius etiam retulit simile monstrū
aridum è Noruegia in Germaniam inferiorem aduectum, marem & fœminam. Fidem ei facere possunt

Marine satyr from **Historia Animalium,**
1585. (By permission of the Folger
Shakespeare Library)

The Middle Ages

The ancient fascination with whales continued into the middle ages. As the countries of western Europe became increasingly skillful at navigating the open seas, the level of their whaling activity increased.

In his *Description of Europe*, the 9th-century Saxon King Alfred touched briefly on the Scandinavian practice of herding whales into fjords, repeating the claim of one Norse nobleman that he and five companions had captured 60 whales in two days using that method. Less than a century later, the Norwegians had transplanted their whaling tradition to Iceland, and by the early 1100s a successful colony had been established on the southwestern coast of Greenland. The Greenlanders supported themselves partly through summer whaling voyages that took them up the Davis Straits and into Baffin Bay in pursuit of migrating whales.

Most information about European attitudes toward whales in this period comes from Scandinavian sagas and other writings, particularly the Norwegian *Speculum Regale*, written in the 13th century. It gives an account of the various species of whales found in the seas around Iceland and discusses the importance of whales to the culture and economy of Norway. Like Pliny's *Naturalis historia*, the *Speculum Regale* is a compilation of tales from many sources, and it presents images of whales distorted by exaggeration, fear, and prejudice.

Speculum Regale describes orca whales as having "teeth like dogs" and as "aggressive to other whales as dogs are to other animals." It relates reports of orcas banding together to attack large baleen whales, biting and exhausting them to the point of death. The narrative notes that many orcas themselves died in these encounters, victims of the flukes of the bigger whales.

The manuscript describes the benign right whale that "does no harm to ships: it has no teeth, and is a fat fish and well edible." It was thought to live very cleanly since, in the absence of teeth, "it does not eat anything except rain and darkness that falls on the sea." This misconception about cetacean diet may also have stemmed from the fact that when stranded right whales were cut open, their stomachs and intestines were devoid of anything even remotely recognizable as food. It would have been difficult to find traces of the small phytoplankton and zooplankton that right whales eat, and the task was complicated by the assumption that such a large creature would require large prey. This idea remained common for some time. A print of the 16th century depicts the battle between a large whale and a giant crustacean of equal size. Presumably the artist had been told that some species of whales fed on shrimp and assumed that any shrimp large enough to satisfy a cetacean appetite would be large indeed.

Speculum Regale tells of frightening sea monsters, often considered to be wicked whales. Many early paintings and woodcuttings of whales show monsters with the heads of pigs and horses, and period literature contains frequent references to pig whales, horse whales, even red whales, all of them evil creatures

> full of greed and fierceness. They are never satisfied in their killing as they ply the oceans looking for ships. They leap into the air so they can move easily, sink the ships and totally destroy them. Those fish are not edible and on the contrary are destined to be the enemies of mankind.

As might be imagined, reports like these did little to ease the apprehensions of people who made their living from the sea. Icelandic sailors shipped out in fear of "bad whales," and even mentioning the word "whale" on board ship was often forbidden in the belief that it would attract the renegades. All whales were referred to as "great fish," and the sailor caught uttering the prohibited word went without food as punishment.

Belue ajarine.

Killer whale battle as imagined by Matthew Paris, around 1250. Paris was a monk whose handwritten **Chronica Majora** recounted highlights of English and European history up to the time of Henry III. In 1241, eleven orca carcasses covered with toothmarks had washed ashore in southeastern England. **Chronica Majora** provided a purely conjectural description of the battle that most of Paris's contemporaries felt certain had caused the whales' deaths.

A crew of flensers has made substantial progress in this plate from Konrad Gesner's **Icones Animalium**, which appeared in 1560. Gesner knew a great deal more about the flensing process than he did about the whale itself. The mouth, eyes, and smokestack-like blowholes are all incorrect, and the tail clearly belongs to a fish. Gesner probably never saw a whale and pieced together this and other pictures from material in books and descriptions supplied by travelers. (By permission of the Folger Shakespeare Library)

Balæna erecta grandem nauem submergens. Videntur & alia quædam Cete ex eâdem Tabula Balænis adnumeranda,quæ ipse simpliciter Cete nominat,cum præter magnitudinem Balænis præcipuè conuenientem , nullam in se corporis partem raram aut monstrosam habeant:ut sunt quæ sequuntur aliqua.

Cetus ingens,quem incolæ Faræ insulæ ichthyophagi,tempestatibus appulsum,unco comprehensum ferreo,securibus dissecant,& partiuntur inter se.

Nauta

The Female Whale

Gesner's engravings became some of the most durable images of whales in Europe. This version of the **Icones** flensing scene appeared 134 years later in a French treatise on pharmaceuticals. Although the arrangement is reversed, everything else is the same, down to the piper standing on the whale's rostrum. (By permission of the Folger Shakespeare Library)

Norwegian fishermen believed that good whales actually herded fish from the open sea, making it unnecessary for them to risk their lives by venturing far from shore. The whales would do this only if the fishermen themselves got along together. If they fell to bickering, the whales would cease helping them. The myth of the whale thus served a useful social function.

The abundance of whales in the waters off Iceland greatly impressed the early Norwegian colonists. According to the *Laxdaela* saga, the whales and the security whaling provided were the incentives that led to the island's settlement. As early as 1281, laws regulating some aspects of whaling were drafted, and many of them remain in effect today. These laws reflected a popular respect for whales comparable to the feelings of native North Americans for the buffalo.

Konrad Gesner, a Swiss doctor who had never seen a whale, published an encyclopedic series of zoological folios beginning in the 1560s. Gesner's treatment of whales did much to reinforce general misconceptions about the animals and some of their sea-monster associates, real or imagined. Gesner created his "whales" using descriptions and prints produced by observers who frequently did not understand what they had seen. His whales have enormous tusks for teeth, baleens around the neck, blowholes like smokestacks growing out of the head, and stubby forelegs and paws. Gesner evidently took the descriptions of sperms, bowheads, and even walruses, and lumped them into a single fearsome beast.

Reports of the size of whales were frequently as exaggerated as reports of their deeds during the middle ages. Numerous folk tales contain variations of a story in which a crew mistakes a slumbering whale for an island, anchors its ship alongside, and sets up camp on its back, sometimes even building a fire. Eventually, the whale awakens and drags crew, camp, and ship to the bottom. Such a legend from 6th-century Ireland concerns Saint Brendon, who not only set up camp on a sleeping whale, but celebrated Mass there with his crew. In honor of the cleric's escape, the mythic island for which he had been searching was named after him, but it was never found.

These embroidered stories involve only orcas, sperm, and large baleen whales, or imagined Gesnerian combinations of them all. Throughout this period, dolphins were still considered lucky omens, lifesaving friends, and even, in the court of England's King Henry VIII, excellent eating.

Early Whaling

Before the 16th century, most whaling was carried out by crews of hunters in light shore-based canoes equipped with small harpoons, nets, or poison-tipped darts. These whalingmen concentrated on the smaller whales for two very practical reasons. Although valuable to an entire village when beached, a large whale was difficult and dangerous to catch. Additionally, in temperate and tropical regions, the bulk of large whales rotted before it could be put to use.

The Japanese used nets to catch large baleen whales in a process that required an impressive level of coordination among the hunters. After surrounding a whale, the hunters would beat loudly on the sides of their boats to confuse the animal and drop large handheld nets between the boats to prevent its escape. Although the whale could easily have broken through these nets, its echolocation may not have conveyed that fact. A trapped whale might have sensed only that obstacles blocked its path in every direction. When the encircling boats had maneuvered the whale close to shore, some of the hunters withdrew to create a path of "escape" that led straight into a maze of 40 nets anchored in shallow water and each measuring 42 m by 33 m (about 140 by 110 ft).

Once the whale was trapped in the stationary nets, lancers paddled in quickly to make initial wounds. As many as 100 thrusts were necessary to kill a large specimen, whose pain and agony were "terrible enough to make one break into a cold sweat," according to *Illustrations of Whaling*, the earliest printed account of the activity in Japan. Although published in 1829, the book described traditional methods in use for centuries.

In addition to net whaling, the Japanese used methods familiar to most other North Pacific peoples. After being alerted by lookouts, boat crews would set out in pursuit of the whale, which they would attempt to overwhelm with harpoons, lances and floats. (The Whaling Museum, New Bedford, Mass.)

Often it was necessary for a Japanese "catcher" to jump onto the dying animal and cut a hole in its snout through which a rope was looped for use if the whale sank. This was often a long procedure, requiring much underwater time. When the hole was complete, a second catcher swam over and secured the rope through the hole. Catchers could always be distinguished from the rest of the crew by their two long braids of hair. If the work of cutting the hole so exhausted the catcher that he could not swim, fellow crewmen would grab him by the braids and pull him back to the boat.

When the whale finally died, the crew chanted three times, "May its soul rest in peace," and thanked Buddha for the prize. They were especially pleased when they had subdued a right whale, not only because its carcass floated, but because its high oil content and baleen made it especially valuable.

When safely ashore, the catchers lined up and performed an animated, heavily ritualized dance in which they reenacted the hunt in mime, teasing each other for lack of bravery or praising special acts of courage. The village also held a memorial service for the dead whale, in which they thanked Buddha for bringing the whale, lamented the need to kill for food, and prayed for the whale's happiness in the afterlife.

There is persuasive evidence to suggest that versions of some of these practices were observed across the North Pacific, from northeast Asia to Alaska and the western coast of North America, until well after Europeans arrived in the 16th century.

Whalers and whale form the seal of the town of Biarritz, 1351. Whaling in the Bay of Biscay was an important transitional phase between whaling for subsistence and the commercial trade that first developed in the Netherlands. Basque whaling never approached the scale of 17th-century Dutch operations, but the Basques found many commercial outlets for whale products. Whale meat appeared often in the markets of most towns along the Biscayan coast; salted blubber was transported to central and eastern France for sale; oil found its way to England for use in soapmaking; and baleen was in demand for many uses in several countries.

In Europe, the oldest records of Basque whaling are from the 11th century, by which time it was firmly established along the Bay of Biscay. As suggested earlier, this whaling tradition may have stretched back to the bone harpoons of 16,000 BC. When right whales began arriving in the fall at the end of their migration from Arctic waters, the Basques posted lookouts in stone towers they had built along the hilltops lining the Bay. Throughout the winter, whenever a whale was sighted, the lookout lit a smoky fire to alert the nearest villages, from which fishermen set out in small boats, or shallops, to chase the whale. This was hazardous work, and luck played an important role, but if the crews succeeded in killing a whale, they towed it back to shore where its blubber was stripped off and carefully divided among the hunters and village members. In some towns, tithe portions were reserved for the Spanish ruler nominally in control of the area.

The Basques were more than a historic footnote to whaling. In a broad sense, they developed the techniques and tools on which all subsequent European whaling was based. The mastery of Basque technology — through training and copying of equipment — became a key to success in the Arctic fishery in the 17th and 18th centuries. The Basques also pioneered two innovations that transformed the nature of whaling. One was pelagic (open-ocean) whaling, and the other was development of the tryworks.

During the 14th century, the Basques began venturing more than a day's sail from shore in search of whales, probably because they had drastically reduced the number of whales wintering in the Bay of Biscay. This required larger, sturdier, and better-equipped vessels, along with a method of preserving blubber for the longer trips. The Basques developed the prototype of the caravel, a sailing ship used on Spanish and Portuguese voyages of discovery in the 15th and 16th centuries. These initial versions were 15-20 m (50-60 ft) long with high sides and a steep poop deck resembling a small castle. Basque whalers very likely began sailing these ships on the path of the right whales' summer migration to the North Sea, where plankton and krill were plentiful. From the Scandinavians they encountered there, the Basques probably learned of the route to Iceland and Greenland, which were already settled and where whales were plentiful.

From Greenland and the Davis Straits, the sail to Newfoundland and North America was a relatively short one. The Basques may have reached the fishing banks and whaling grounds there over 100 years before Columbus sailed. The oldest surviving record of Basque visits to the Grand Banks, however, dates from the early 1540s. In 1578 an English observer reported that among 350 vessels fishing for cod off the coast of Newfoundland, 100 were Basque, and they were accompanied by 30 additional Basque vessels engaged solely in whaling.

In the late 1590s, the Basques began to adopt a new method of boiling down or "trying out" whale blubber on the whaling ship. They built brick ovens into which were set large iron vats. Once fires were lighted beneath the vats, large batches of the fat stripped from the whale carcass could be cooked down to liquid. The boiling oil was then ladled into cooling troughs and later poured into barrels for storage in the hold.

This innovation enabled the Basque crews to spend more time at sea on each whaling trip, since oil served as a more efficient form of storing fat than did pickled blubber. Shunned by other European nations when they first adopted Basque whaling techniques in the 17th century, the shipboard tryworks became a fundamental element of Yankee whaling in the 19th century.

As the sophistication of whaling technology increased toward the end of the 16th century, economic and social factors in several countries sparked an interest in whaling. In northern Europe and in England, growing merchant classes searched hungrily for new enterprises that would bring them fast profits. Whale oil — valuable for lighting, lubrication, and soapmaking — was an important commodity during the period, and it did not escape the notice of these newly-minted capitalists. The success of the Basques at whaling further stirred their interest. English expeditions sent through the sub-Arctic oceans above Europe discovered not a northeast passage to the Orient, but a route to Russia that passed through rich whaling grounds. This intensified interest in whaling.

This period marked the initial movement away from whaling for subsistence to whaling as an industry creating products for manufacture and international trade. Financial gain became the driving force behind whaling, establishing a pattern that led eventually to the near-fatal overfishing of whale stocks in the late 19th and early 20th centuries.

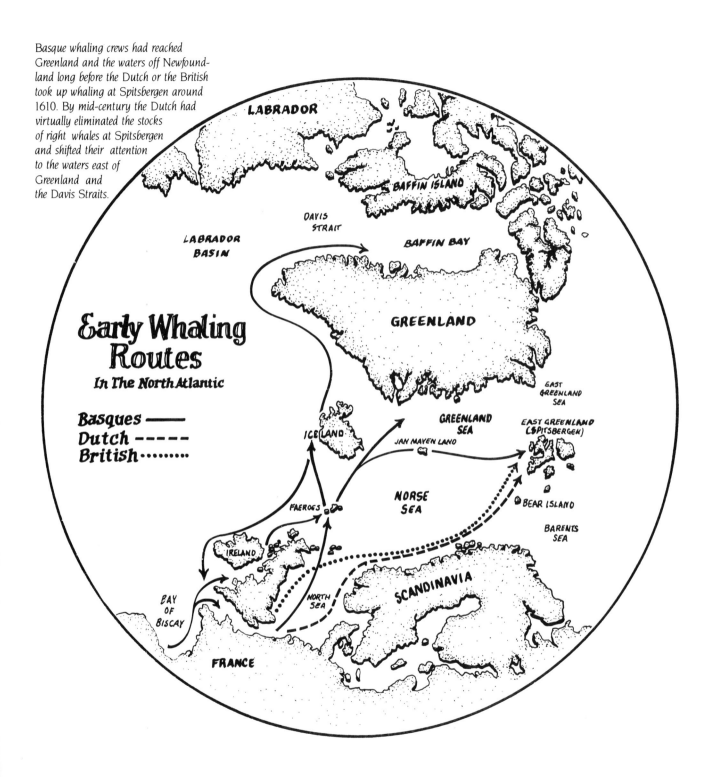

Basque whaling crews had reached Greenland and the waters off Newfoundland long before the Dutch or the British took up whaling at Spitsbergen around 1610. By mid-century the Dutch had virtually eliminated the stocks of right whales at Spitsbergen and shifted their attention to the waters east of Greenland and the Davis Straits.

LABRADOR

BAFFIN ISLAND

DAVIS STRAIT

LABRADOR BASIN

BAFFIN BAY

GREENLAND

EAST GREENLAND SEA

Early Whaling Routes
In The North Atlantic

Basques ———
Dutch - - - - -
British ·········

GREENLAND SEA

EAST GREENLAND (=SPITSBERGEN)

JAN MAYEN LAND

ICELAND

BEAR ISLAND

FAEROES

NORSE SEA

BARENTS SEA

IRELAND

SCANDINAVIA

BAY OF BISCAY

NORTH SEA

FRANCE

Britain's Muscovy Company, a speculative trading association encouraged by the Crown, was the first commercial whaling venture. It existed on paper from 1557, but it was only after a major reorganization and the granting of a royal monopoly on whaling that capital could be raised to finance its initial exploratory voyage in 1604.

This was the first of a series of expeditions the company sent to Bear and Spitsbergen Islands between Norway and Greenland. Both the British and the Dutch claimed to have discovered Spitsbergen and its whale-rich waters. As a result, the first 20 years of northern ocean whaling in Europe were marked by international fighting, complete with sabotage of competing whaling vessels and, later, government-sponsored military convoys for some of the whaling fleets.

Despite such hazards, ships from all over Europe began to arrive at Spitsbergen during the summer season. They included Basque, French, and German crews, and

Three Dutch ships docked at a busy shore processing station around 1780. The tryworks is at center, and the worker at left on top ladles the clarified oil into a keg for storage. (Hart Nautical Museum, Massachusetts Institute of Technology)

unauthorized private vessels from Britain and the Netherlands. The strength of Dutch military escorts secured for the Dutch monopoly company the right to work the waters and bays of Spitsbergen by the early 1620s, and they lost no time in taking advantage of the situation. In 1622 they introduced an important innovation with the construction of the first "blubbertown," which they called Smeerenburg from their word for fat, *smeer.* Coastal whalers had always thrown up temporary structures to house the vats and furnaces used in trying out the blubber once the whales were brought to shore; but the Dutch actually created a town at the site of the harvest. Other nations followed suit, and blubbertowns sprang up along the bays of Spitsbergen, West Spitsbergen, and Bear Islands.

At its peak, 18,000 people were said to be employed each summer at Smeerenburg, with as many as 300 ships anchored within range of its blubberhouses. Although these figures have been questioned by modern researchers — since Smeerenburg was only used in summer, all 18,000 people would have required transport to and from the Netherlands each year — the larger prosperity of whaling as an industry during this period is not in doubt. In 1620, the "whalebone" (baleen) and oil of a single right whale could be sold for $12,000 in Europe, or twice the cost of outfitting a single whale ship. The baleen provided stiffening for clothing and served as an ideal material for early clock springs; the oil was used for lighting and in the making of soap and the tanning of leather.

By the end of the 1620s the whaling industry employed thousands across Europe in supporting occupations — bakers, vintners, bookkeepers, coopers, tobacconists and artisans of all sorts — as well as the workers directly involved in the actual processing. The bulk of these jobs were located in the Netherlands, which had leaped to the forefront of European whaling by the end of the decade. With vast commercial fleets, great amounts of capital for investment, consistent government support, and superior skill at learning the Basque whaling techniques, the Dutch dominated European pelagic whaling for nearly 150 years.

Competition remained fierce, and England was among the first casualties. Unable to match the technological skill and financial backing of the Dutch, the English fleet slid into internal bickering. As early as 1630, English whaling was in serious decline and no longer posed any threat to the Dutch or the Basques.

Depletion of the whale stocks around Spitsbergen toward the mid-17th century forced ships to travel farther from land, well into the sub-Arctic seas. This forced a gradual shift to pelagic whaling, following the pattern established by the Basques in the previous century. The pre-eminent Dutch moved west, first to the waters off the eastern coast of Greenland, and by the end of the century to the Davis Straits on that island's western side. Blubbertowns could not be built on the shifting ice fields in these seas, so blubber had to be preserved until the ships could return to port. Although the Basques had pioneered the use of shipboard tryworks, whaling crews resisted adopting this technique because of the danger fire posed to a wooden ship. Under these circumstances, the whaling crews gradually developed more effective methods of removing and storing the blubber.

In preparation for stripping, the carcass was hoisted up alongside the whaleboat and flensed as it hung there. This required that the flensers actually stand on the carcass which, though suspended horizontally, was extremely slippery. The blubber was peeled off in huge strips called "blankets." Once on board, the blankets were chopped into smaller pieces, pickled, and packed away in large barrels. This was a messy process, and the abandoned whale carcasses often attracted sharks. On occasion, flensers lost their footing on the whale's oily back and tumbled into the icy water to become a splendid meal for the waiting sharks.

By the late 17th century, whaling efforts had begun in America but were confined to beachings and scattered coastal hunting parties. In 1711, the capture of a sperm whale in the ocean south of Nantucket launched a period of rapid growth in American whaling. The residents of resource-poor Nantucket enthusiastically took to the new trade as a source of income, and they quickly rose to dominance in the colonial industry. Although Nantucket remained the capital of American whaling for over a century, other harbor towns entered the trade. By the time of the colonial revolt against Britain, active whaling ports stretched along the New England coast and included Gloucester, Salem, Marblehead, Provincetown, Martha's Vineyard, and New Bedford in Massachusetts; Newport, Rhode Island; New London, Mystic and Stonington in Connecticut; and Sag Harbor and the Hamptons on Long Island. At the close of the 18th century, Yankee ships were sailing to whaling grounds and ports stretching from the tips of South America and southern Africa to Canada and the Greenland fishery.

Illustration from an account of whaling off Greenland, published in London in 1704. At D, five shallops have formed a line to haul a carcass to the temporary shore station in the background at B. (By permission of the Folger Shakespeare Library)

Many whalingmen respected whales as formidable opponents in a dangerous but profitable contest. Some foresaw the decline of whales and lamented the extermination of such noble animals. But there was money to be made, and the whale's capacity for destruction could mean loss of life or profit (which was worse in the eyes of many shipowners). William Scoresby, a British scientist who spent twenty years as a crew member and ship captain in the whaling trade, expressed the essential ambivalence of whalingmen toward their prey. "There is something extremely painful in the destruction of a whale," he wrote, "yet the object of the adventure, the value of the prize, the joy of the capture, cannot be sacrificed for feelings of compassion."

American whaling prospered in the first half of the 19th century. During a 40-year "golden age" that began after the War of 1812, Yankee ships dominated the industry. Their success was due in part to sheer numbers; for every whaler that left any port elsewhere in the world, four put out from New England. Most of these ships headed south to the Portuguese Azores and Cape Verde Islands where they hired experienced harpooners, considered the best in the business. Many of the islanders made the return trip to New England and ultimately settled there. Today, nearly 80% of the population of New Bedford, Massachusetts, is of Portuguese descent. When whaling collapsed, the Portuguese turned to other ways of making a living from the sea, and became the backbone of the New England fishing industry. (Interestingly, a limited sperm whale fishery continues in the Azores, where the whalingmen still use hand-thrown harpoons.)

Once the ship reached the whaling ground, the search for whales began. A spotter climbed into the "crows nest," a metal barrel hoop attached to the mast. When he spotted a whale or its spout on the horizon, he alerted the crew with the cry "Thar' she blows!" He shouted approximate location and distance to guide the other men as they lowered the small catcher boats lashed to the sides of the ship. Much of the crew left, but the spotter remained aloft to relay locations. To avoid shouting across great distances of water, complicated signal systems were devised that included raising and lowering flags and adjusting the sails.

The catcher boats were 9 m (30 ft) long — essentially the length of aboriginal whaling canoes — 2 m (6 ft) wide, and extremely narrow at each end. They were equipped with sails for speed when closing in on the animals, but once the boats neared the whales, oars were used for control and maneuverability. Four men rowed the boat, a steerer sat in the stern, and a harpooner, armed with a harpoon (and later, a shoulder gun) sat in the bow. A rope attached to the harpoon and tied to a post in the stern lay coiled in the bow. When the whale was harpooned it sped off in an effort to escape, dragging the boat behind it on a short, wild trip that whalingmen dubbed a "Nantucket sleigh ride." As the whale tired, more harpoons were thrown. Eventually, a lance or a shot from the shoulder gun killed the animal by piercing its heart and lungs. The dead whale was towed back to the mother ship for processing.

Whalingmen learned quickly that many species of whales seem to have tight social orders and family structures. They discovered that a mother would rarely abandon her injured calf, so they would harpoon the calf first and then the mother. Larger whales occasionally capsized the small catcher boats in agony or anger, but in only a handful of cases did the same thing happen to a large mother vessel. The best known instance occured in 1820, when a wounded sperm whale rammed the Nantucket ship *Essex* several hundred miles off the coast of Peru. She went down in less than 30 minutes, and only five crew members survived three months at sea in small catcher boats. An account of the sinking provided Herman Melville with a model for parts of *Moby Dick*, which appeared over 20 years later.

The golden age of Yankee whaling was not quite so golden for Yankee whalingmen. Life aboard the ships was strenuous, uncomfortable, and hardly the romance that legend has painted it. The crew lived in the perpetually damp forecastle, a cramped section deep in the ship with 1.5 m (5 ft) of head space. Portholes did not exist, and the number of oil lamps was restricted in the interest of safety, leaving the quarters in semi-darkness even at midday. The narrow bunks, built in two levels around the space, were short, padded with straw, and frequently infested with lice and fleas. Conditions in the other living space, the "'tween deck," were comparable. The leaky deck dripped water constantly, and there was little hope of clothes, bedding, or possessions ever drying.

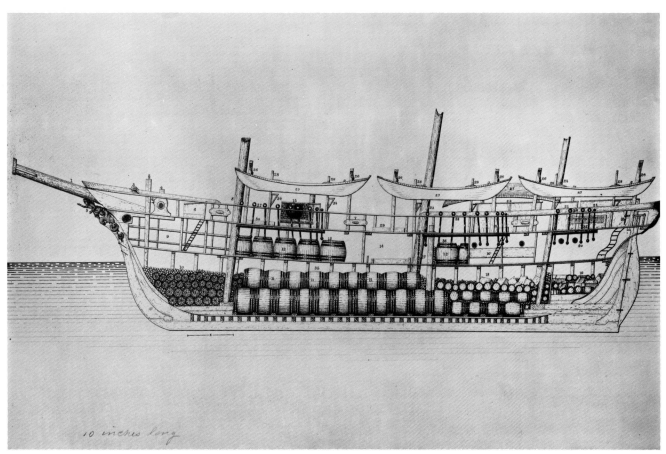

10 inches long

A cutaway view of the American whaleship **Alice Knowles.** *Starting at the top, note the three whaleboats in their davits (27, 26); the iron caldron and brick frame of the tryworks (15); and barrels for storing oil (11). Every available space in the hold has been filled with cordwood for firing the tryworks (10, 35, 18, 19, 36), and the ship's entire supply of drinking water is stored elsewhere in barrels. (Smithsonian Institution photo)*

Meals were worse. Fresh food became a memory three days out of port as only the most imperishable provisions could be stored for any length of time. Mealworms appeared in the stale biscuits. Dried beans, peas, onions and potatoes were staples, to be made into endless stews with heavily salted meats.

The work itself was wet, smelly and slippery. Any washing of bodies or clothing was done in saltwater since the small amount of fresh water aboard had to be rationed carefully for drinking and cooking. Clothes were hung to dry in the damp sea breeze.

Despite the absence of glamour, men still lined up for positions on the whaling ships. Young boys yearning to break free of the family farm were easily lured by stories of adventure on the high seas. These boys, some not even in their teens, often arrived at the dock ill-prepared for a year's voyage that might take them into polar regions. The clothes they wore could not provide protection or last long even

Cutting up a sperm whale on the American whaleship California *in 1903. The crew members work from a stage attached to the ship's side, a piece of equipment 17th-century whalingmen did not have, but otherwise the work differs little from the work of 1673. Crewmen cut off the lower jaw, which is removed and hoisted in. The teeth will provide whale ivory for carving (scrimshaw), and the bone may be ground for fertilizer. (The Whaling Museum, New Bedford, Mass.)*

under ideal conditions. When a whalingman died at sea, his sea chest was opened and the belongings bartered off. Young men who had signed on without fit clothing were often "given" extra clothing. These boys were poorly paid to begin with, and the captain kept a close accounting of what was handed out to them. At the end of a year's cruise, an exhausted, homesick boy was often told not only that he had no wages coming, but that he owed the captain another cruise in payment of debts.

Reports of the day are almost unanimous in describing the crews as cheerful and enthusiastic in spite of such poor living and working conditions. Even when a ship broke up on the ice, the crew was found "happy as larks," according to one journal. Crews heading into the tropics fared somewhat better than others. Stops at the islands meant time on land, fresh fruit and water, and some social life. Eager replacements for whalemen who had died or jumped ship were plentiful among many of the island societies.

Stiff in their civilian clothes, three New Bedford whalingmen pose for a portrait around 1880. The crews of 19th-century American whaling ships were notable for their racial diversity. In addition to young New Englanders of western European stock, a crew might include Azoreans, Cape Verdean blacks, Orientals, Pacific Islanders, Native Americans from both North and South America, and Eskimos. Of these groups, the Portuguese-speaking Africans were considered most skillful at whaling. As the industry declined in the late 19th century, they came into possession of several aging whaleships. According to one whaling history, most of the 28 ships operating out of New England in 1906 were controlled by this group, who continued to hunt in the 19th-century manner long after the rest of the world's whaling nations had "progressed" to more modern methods.

Part of the Stone Fleet sinks at Savannah in early 1862. The Union purchased 40 New England whaleships, most already in poor repair, in the autumn of 1861. The ships were scuttled in the harbors at Charleston and Savannah in an effort to halt blockade-running there, but tidal action quickly broke them apart. The Civil War helped end the "golden age" of American whaling and contributed directly to the industry's later decline. By 1865, a combination of direct destruction (the Stone Fleet plan, privateers) and conversion to other uses had cut the whaling fleet in half.

Through his writing, Melville helped bestow mythic status on these New Englanders and their trade, but the way of life he immortalized in *Moby Dick* and other stories vanished almost as soon as it had appeared. Within 20 years of the novel's appearance, American whaling was dying, a victim of the shocks of war, economic adversity, and declining stocks.

Initially, the most significant of these problems was the Civil War, which led to the destruction of one-half of the great whaling ships. Some were converted to warships and nearly 50 destroyed by marauding Confederate privateers. In an effort to tighten its blockade of southern ports, the Union purchased 40 aging New Bedford whalers in 1861, filled them with rubble, and sailed them into the harbors at Charleston and Savannah where they were sunk. The "stone fleet" tactic proved ineffective, however, and shipping out of both ports continued undisturbed.

More serious problems appeared after the war. In the late 1850s, petroleum had been discovered in Pennsylvania. In the years following the war it began to replace whale oil as the primary fuel for artificial illumination. But the overriding difficulty was the depletion of traditional whale populations. As stocks disappeared in one area after another, whaling crews were forced to travel farther from port to find

them. Completion of a transcontinental railway in 1869 encouraged establishment of west coast whaling operations that could ship products to eastern markets. This opened the fishery for gray whales off the California coast, but they were soon as scarce as sperms and rights on the east coast. The west coast whalers responded by sailing further north into the Arctic, where they ran increasing risks of damage from ice and bad weather. American whaling in the North Pacific suffered a major setback in the summer of 1871 when ice trapped most of the fleet, and 34 vessels were crushed or damaged beyond repair. Packed into small harpoon boats, the crew members drifted 130 kilometers (80 mi) until they were rescued by the remaining 7 vessels. Miraculously, not a single hand was lost. A total of 2100 men arrived safely in Honolulu that autumn, but the North Pacific fleet never recovered.

World War I effectively brought American whaling to an end in the Pacific. On the Atlantic coast, the sperm whales that had been the industry's mainstay were, like most familiar whale populations by the late 1800s, seriously depleted. In 1924, the schooner *Wanderer* put out of New Bedford only to be wrecked within miles of port. Her loss marked the end of America's whaling industry.

Modern Whaling

Even as the whaling industry in America and other nations slipped into decline, a Norwegian's persistent search for technological answers to traditional whaling problems began to pay off. Beginning in the 1860s, refinements developed by Svend Foyn revived the industry for Norway and Britain and later Russia and Japan. But the changes also introduced a deadly, relentless form of hunt that pushed one species of whale after another to the edge of extinction in the 20th century.

Each of Foyn's three major changes actually involved modifications of traditional whaling methods with technology borrowed from other areas. First, Foyn experimented with designs for a motorized catcher boat to replace the small, oar-powered shallops in which whaling crews traditionally chased their prey. In 1868 he launched a boat, the 29-meter (94-foot) *Spes et Fides*, capable of traveling at 7 knots. On board the vessel were two significant new features. One was a bow-mounted cannon that shot a combined harpoon and bomb lance. The harpoon's umbrella-like barbs opened on impact and broke a vial of acid that ignited a gunpowder charge. The other feature provided a system of springs and pulleys, called an accumulator, that dispersed the strain on the harpoon line created by a struggling whale. These two modifications increased the number of whales a boat could kill while sharply cutting the proportion of carcasses it lost.

In 1868, the *Spes et Fides* caught 38 rorquals. It was an astonishing haul for one season, and it showed how decisively the deadly catcher boats would alter whaling. The new boats spread rapidly through the Norwegian fleet. Whaling crews could now keep pace with the swift rorquals that had previously eluded men in sail- and oar-powered boats, and the motorized catchers proved sturdy enough to reach the final retreats of several whale species in the icy Arctic.

All of this meant substantially increased takes and a new problem for the whaling crews: catches now overhwelmed the mother ships served by the new catcher boats. Flensing and trying out could not be done on board with so many whales coming in. The Norwegians chose once more to mechanize a traditional whaling technique in response to a new problem. They began to build onshore processing stations no different, in principle, from the blubbertown built by the Dutch at Smeerenburg 250 years earlier. Mechanization began to work its way through the whaling industry, both causing and accommodating a vast new scale of operation.

The Norwegians initially worked their own coastal waters with notable success. In 1885, for example, they killed 1398 whales, and the following year, fishing the coast of Finmark in the extreme north, they claimed 895 whales. Technological refinements continued to increase the whalers' effective range as they cut into whale populations close to home ports. Norwegian whaling crews began to range farther from port, and the shipowners, now organizing as large firms, established a far-flung network of shore stations. Here whales were reduced to their marketable constituents — oil for lubrication, bone and meat for fertilizer — and shipped to Europe. The progression of land stations marked the trail of whale stocks all but exterminated by Norwegian whaling: Iceland, Newfoundland, Spain, South Africa, Australia, and South America.

Following Norway's lead, the British, Russians, Japanese and French entered the modern era with mechanized boats and equipment, and networks of whaling stations. The British undertook the most sizable operations, establishing stations in Ireland, Scotland, and Gibraltar, and followed the Norwegians into the Antarctic after 1908. By 1910, North Atlantic whale stocks had fallen off so dramatically that expansion into other regions was the only choice left to whaling firms. This

(right) Harpoon cannon with a "cold" (nonexplosive) tip mounted on an Icelandic catcher boat. (Greenpeace photo)

imposed new financial and logistical pressures that ultimately led to an even more intense pursuit of whales. By the outbreak of World War I, the greatest of the whale species were being hunted relentlessly worldwide.

The move to modernization was not as smooth as it appears in hindsight. The American industry continued to decline because of its fixation on certain whale species — primarily the vanishing sperm — and a refusal to abandon the sailing ship for more modern hunting methods. The development of substitutes for a range of whale products also contributed to the decline. Resource-rich America could afford to turn its attention to other industrial pursuits.

In Britain there was also much resistance to new ideas about whaling. By 1892 unmotorized vessels were so unsuited for hunting the vanishing North Atlantic whales, that four of Britain's largest remaining sail-powered whaleships moved south to the Antarctic in search of the relatively slow right whales. Even this desperate move failed, largely because American whaling crews had nearly wiped out the southern right whale. Unable to catch the quicker rorqual species, the four vessels resorted to raiding seal colonies. After the expedition's return, three Scottish naturalists who had sailed with it tried unsuccessfully to muster enthusiasm for mechanizing Britain's industry along Norwegian lines. Industrialists and financiers, deterred by the costs of modernization and fluctuations in prices for whale oil, were as yet unwilling to admit that the traditional methods were inadequate.

The continuing decline of whale stocks in the North Atlantic ultimately forced the decision on them, and in the familiar pattern of the period, it was Norway that took the lead. Beginning in the 1890s, the Norwegian C. A. Larson made repeated trips to the Antarctic on sealing and scientific expeditions. By 1903, he had developed plans for a whaling station based on South Georgia, one of the Falkland Islands east of Tierra del Fuego. In 1904, he established his station with Argentine financing. Whaling in the protected cove he chose for his station was so effortless that for months the crew filled its quota without leaving the harbor. The abundance of whales, especially the slow humpbacks, and the premium price for oil encouraged wasteful hunting and processing methods. Hundreds of carcasses were set adrift after only partial processing, causing the loss of tons of oil.

Although these whales soon dwindled, Larson's company registered a profit in its third season. The initial return was so large that it touched off a rush of lease applications to the British, who controlled the Falklands. Whaling companies, primarily Norwegian, scrambled for entry into the Antarctic whale fishery. They ignored the possibility that increased competition for a finite stock of whales would force profits to decline.

In one of the earliest attempts to discourage wasteful whaling practices, Britain limited the number of licenses granted for the island, but by 1911, eight leases had been issued to six companies. Other companies were forced to work from South Shetland and South Orkney, neither of which offered land sites or whales of equivalent value.

The dearth of good locations for processing stations, and the annoyances of the leasing procedure, encouraged still another revolutionizing technological step, again from Norway. It was the floating factory ship, initially an old merchant vessel refitted with a modern tryworks and industrial pressure cookers for other products. Through the late 1920s, these ships anchored in protected bays of South Atlantic islands and operated as bases for fleets of catcher boats. Procedures on the floating factory were similiar to those of shore stations. The whales were hauled through a slipway onto the deck where they were cut up and tried out. Oil, baleen, and meat (increasingly popular as fertilizer) were stored for the return to port.

Yankee whaling was well into its decline when this picture of the New Bedford harbor was taken in 1882. Even though the Norwegians were already earning huge profits with the new steam-powered catcher boats, Americans clung to sailing ships. Dwindling whale stocks, the increasing use of petroleum for lighting, and the ravages of the Civil War all contributed to the collapse of the American industry. And for New Bedford, an added indignity: in the 1870s San Francisco became the primary American whaling port because of its proximity to the (relatively) abundant Arctic grounds — which were soon exhausted.

Svend Foyn revolutionized whaling in Norway by the judicious application of mechanization to traditional whaling equipment. The bow-mounted cannon, introduced in the 1860s, was one of his most important innovations. Its exploding harpoon tips and great accuracy dramatically increased the number of whales the Norwegians were able to kill.

Floating factories offered important advantages over land stations. They could travel in response to declining whale stocks or migrations without the complications involved in moving a shore station. Construction costs were significantly lower than for land stations, and the sponsoring government or firm no longer needed to apply for leases. And the floating factories were capable of maintaining the catcher boats that accompanied them. In most cases, the factory vessels were so large that the 37-meter catchers (120 ft) could be hoisted up the slipway for repair.

The catcher boats themselves were refined for greater efficiency. Because the harpoon cannons were ineffective beyond 23 meters (75 ft), it was imperative that the boats be capable of bringing them as close as possible to their targets. As a result, the catchers were designed for maximum maneuverability; with balanced rudders and cut-away sterns, the average catcher boat could execute a complete turn within its own length in about a minute.

By this period, the acid vial in the harpoon had been replaced by a timing device that touched off an explosion seconds after launching. Because the harpoons were often bent beyond service by the struggles of the whale, each factory ship carried a blacksmith to straighten out the steel shafts.

The application of technological refinements continued in the 20th century. Oil-fired catchers were launched by the British in 1923, and oil soon replaced coal as boiler fuel on the steam-powered catchers. In 1937, the Japanese unveiled the first diesel-engine catcher, but it was so noisy that it did not immediately replace steam-powered boats. The din often frightened whales, forcing the catchers to pursue them longer than they normally would.

Today's whale catchers represent even further refinements of these antecedants. They are bigger, heavier, and above all they are faster. With the common 3000-horsepower diesel engine, they can travel at speeds above 20 knots. The swiftest rorquals can exceed 20 knots for short periods, but they lack the endurance to outrun the catchers.

Modern floating factories bear scant resemblance to their predecessors of the early 20th century. They are efficient, self-contained communities, complete with sophisticated navigational equipment and nearly every craftsman a small city would boast, from barbers and carpenters to bakers and mechanics. With their

helicopters, fleets of catcher boats, and cavernous steam cookers for the whale carcasses, they are essentially huge harvesting/processing machines.

The Japanese, now the world's leading whaling nation, learned modern whaling techniques from the Russians late in the 19th century. Net whaling was still common in Japan when Czar Nicholas II set up the Russian Pacific Whaling Company. Its efficient new methods and impressive gross tonnages convinced Jyuro Oka, a Japanese entrepreneur with no whaling background, to establish a similar company in 1889. Based at a net whaling station and equipped with an 11-knot motorized vessel, the new Japanese company took 15 whales the first year, 42 the second, and 60 in the third. Others followed Oka's lead, and the proliferation of modern whaling companies led to the establishment of a chain of stations along Japan's northeast Pacific coast.

The selective appropriation of western technology that established this whaling industry from scratch was typical of Japan's effort to modernize and industrialize itself in the late 19th century. This pattern was repeated in every sector of the economy. When the Japanese had learned all they could from the Russians, they took another characteristic step. They went to the world's masters of modern whaling, the Norwegians, and hired them as consultants to their whaling effort. By the early 20th century, this short period of intensive cultivation had put Japanese whaling far in advance of its Russian counterpart. Japan controlled a network of 40 whaling stations on its own archipelago, in Korea, on Formosa and in the Kuril Islands. An effort to organize these stations ultimately produced two consolidated companies still in existence.

In 1934, the Japanese extended their whaling into the Antarctic. Purchasing a Norwegian floating factory and a small fleet of catchers, they began pursuit of finback and blue whales. Within five years, the two companies jointly controlled a fleet of six floating factories and a full complement of catchers. The Japanese, who refused to adopt the voluntary conservation restrictions other whaling nations accepted in 1931 and 1937, became the pre-eminent nation in the Antarctic.

With southern whaling established, the Japanese moved in 1940 into the North Pacific and the Arctic, but World War II halted expansion there. Most of Japan's fleet was diverted to military use and was subsequently destroyed. Postwar Japan used American financial aid to build a technologically advanced replacement fleet.

There was no escape for the animal above or below the water with the new fleet. Catchers were equipped with sonar to track submerged whales. Later, helicopters were added to the factory vessels, from which they could range in search of widely-scattered clusters of whales. Radio communication directed the catchers and factory boats to the whales.

Mechanization and industrial efficiency have had drastic consequences for both whales and whalingmen. They are the ultimate outcome of the shift in the nature of whaling that took place in 17th-century Europe. Before that time, the whale had been treated solely as a source of food and the raw materials necessary to a hunter's survival. Aboriginal whaling parties were small, and they only killed enough whales to satisfy the needs of their families and villages. Further, they hunted with a strong sense of life as a web connecting all living beings. Many northern Pacific cultures actually conducted ritual lamentations for dead cetaceans.

European nations brought a dramatically different attitude to whaling when they took it up as a trade around 1600. They saw whales strictly in terms of retail products yielded. Financial gain, not basic survival, fired their interest in the hunt. Modern whaling is nothing more than this whale-as-commodity approach amplified by powerful technology. There is little chance of escape from the swift

Icelandic catcher boats in the North Atlantic, 1979. Note the bow-mounted harpoon cannon. Icelandic catchers are based at shore processing stations; in the Soviet and Japanese whaling fleets they work from factory ships that process the catches at sea. The catchers can maintain high speeds long enough to tire fleeing whales, after which they can be killed with relative ease. (Greenpeace photo)

57

catcher boats, no defense against the explosive harpoon. The oceans are now the factory ships' domain, and no species of whale, however swift or small, is exempt from pursuit. In the mindless logic of western economics, there is no end to an activity as long as a market for its products exists. That logic was a relentless hunter when it pursued North American passenger pigeons and bison herds. The same hunter now stalks the whales.

Dead sperm whale being hauled up the slipway of the Soviet factory ship **Dalniy Vostok.** *(William Mosgrove photo, courtesy Greenpeace)*

The Whaling Problem

Natural resources that occur not in any nation's territory but in areas shared by all nations are called common resources. No one owns these resources; they belong to all nations and all people. When competition for a common resource is unrestricted, whoever can exploit it fastest gets the most. There is no financial incentive for restraint. An agreement among all potential exploiters to moderate their use of the resource can assure that each one receives a fair portion. In the absence of such an understanding, each exploiter feels compelled to take as much of the resource as possible to assure that it gets a share before the resource is depleted. If the resource in question is a living one, like fish or whales, then exploiters must agree further to take only the amount that can be produced in a year without depleting the resource. This is called a "sustainable yield." If exploiters fail to reach such an agreement, they will deplete and may exterminate the living resource. Unfortunately, most international agreements to prevent the depletion of common resources have not been successful. This failure is called "the tragedy of the commons," and it is the tragedy that has befallen whales.

Economics is the principal motivation for depleting whale stocks. According to traditional theory of resource conservation and management, whales can and should be harvested at the level of their maximum sustainable yield (MSY). Theoretically, a given stock of animals will reproduce at a rate that varies in relation to population size. At some point — usually midway between maximum potential population and zero population — the rate of reproduction peaks. This is the MSY level. As population rises above this point, the rate of reproduction begins to drop because increasing density subjects the animals to a number of stresses, including limits on the availability of food. The reproduction rate also declines as total population moves in the other direction, in this instance because there are fewer sexually mature animals to produce offspring. MSY thus represents a biologically efficient standard for harvesting whales and other living resources. Yet because it restricts take, MSY limits profits, and therefore, is economically inefficient. There is more money to be made from depleting or exterminating whales than harvesting on an MSY basis.

The Antarctic blue whale provides a useful illustration of this conflict between economics and conservation. Scientists estimate the maximum population at about 150,000. They also suggest 75,000 as a likely MSY level and say that 2,000 whales could probably be taken yearly without depleting them. If the stock is at MSY level and each blue whale is worth $10,000, then the industry can make $20 million per year, not counting expenses. This would represent conservation and management of the stock. But what if the industry were to take all 75,000 whales in one year? That would bring in up to $750 million, which the industry could then invest in other enterprises at a conservative 10% annual return. That would produce $75 million each year, nearly four times the revenue from harvesting at MSY. Even with expenses factored, the economics of whaling impel the industry to take as many whales as possible, as fast as possible, without regard for MSY and the long-term interests of whales and whaling.

This illustration admittedly oversimplifies the situation. The demand for products made from blue whales, for example, would probably drop if the market were glutted in one year, and the $10,000 value per whale would decline correspondingly. The cost of whaling must also be considered. As the number of whales decreases, finding the remaining ones requires increasing amounts of time and money. At some point, it would become too expensive to find the last remaining whales, and

Also any Whale, or such like great fish cast upon any shore, shall be safely kept or improved [processed] where it cannot be kept by the town or other proprietor of the land, till the Generall Court [legislature] shall set Order for the same.
— Massachusetts law, 1641

whaling would stop. In the case of blue whales, however, whalers could focus on other species when one stock was depleted, yet continue to kill the remaining few when the opportunity arose. This is, in fact, exactly what has happened to the blue whale.

The Failure of Conservation

By 1930, modern whaling fleets had taken their toll on whales in every ocean. Traditional whaling grounds in the North Atlantic and eastern Pacific had been exhausted before World War I. The war interrupted whaling and provided a short respite for whale stocks. When the war ended, whaling resumed, and several nations added refitted military ships to their whaling fleets. This increased effort, combined with rapid advances in technological efficiency, added to pressures on remaining whale stocks. In 1931, nearly 200 catcher boats serving 38 factory ships slaughtered over 42,000 great whales in the Antarctic alone.

It required no great insight to see that whale stocks could not long sustain such intense hunting. Limits were needed if whaling were to continue on a long-term basis. Working through the League of Nations, the United States pressed for an international agreement to impose such limits, and in 1931, 22 nations signed the Geneva Convention for the Regulation of Whaling. Two major whaling nations — Japan and Russia — were not among them.

Although the Geneva Convention provided only minimal regulation, it was the first agreement on whaling, and it established important precedents for later international accords. Its range was limited: restrictions applied to baleen whales only, excluding the sperm whale and other toothed species. Right whales, already depleted, were given complete protection, and the pact excused from its coverage subsistence whaling conducted by aboriginal peoples when they used traditional hunting techniques. It prohibited the taking of calves, immature whales, and females with calves, and imposed other restrictions designed to discourage disruption of the reproductive cycle. The convention required that the fullest possible use be made of whale carcasses to avoid wasteful practices; that whaling vessels register with the nation under whose flag they operated; and that each nation supply the International Bureau of Whaling Statistics in Norway with data and basic biological information about whales taken by its fleet. Most important, the Convention applied to "all the waters of the world, including both the high seas and territorial and national waters." Significantly, the agreement lacked any enforcement provision. It relied on individual nations to impose the regulations on their own whaling vessels and to police their own waters.

Given its limited scope, the Convention had little effect on the increasing overexploitation of whales during the 1930s. Land-based whaling decimated coastal stocks, and Antarctic whaling expanded as nations rushed for their share of the resource. This was the period of Japan's entry into Antarctic whaling, a significant expansion of effort there. But Japan, like the Soviet Union, still refused to sign the Convention. To many observers the whaling industry was heading for a disaster — extermination of stocks — unless tougher regulations could be imposed.

In 1937, nine nations met in London to sign a more restrictive, though still insufficient, agreement to regulate whaling. Signatory nations included South Africa, Argentina, Germany, the United Kingdom, Ireland, New Zealand and the United States. Japan and the Soviet Union were again conspicuous in their refusal to sign.

The 1937 Convention broadened the scope of the 1931 agreement. Its provisions

"In 1931 nearly 200 catcher boats serving 38 factory ships slaughtered over 42,000 great whales in the Antarctic alone."

applied to sperm and baleen whales and extended total protection to a second species, the gray whales (which were already receiving partial protection under a U.S.-Mexican treaty signed in 1936). All factory ships and land stations operating under the flags of signatory nations were specifically included. Of most importance, the 1937 Convention set minimum size limits for blue, fin, humpback, and sperm whales, and established closed areas and seasons for factory ships and land stations. The area and season restrictions were designed to protect whales during calving, to provide sanctuaries where whales would not be disturbed, to close areas where whales were already depleted, and to limit the overall whaling effort without cutting any nation's individual effort. The regulations were a significant advance, but the signatory nations acknowledged that additional constraints would probably be necessary.

Specifically, the 1937 Convention distinguished between pelagic or factory-ship whaling and coastal whaling. Because factory ships can pursue whales anywhere, pelagic whaling deprives whales of any refuge. In contrast, the range of land-based catcher boats is limited, and whales can reach relative safety after running the gauntlet of coastal whaling ships. But there are other significant distinctions. Particularly in equatorial regions, land stations are more wasteful than factory ships because the migrating whales they take generally carry less fat — and consequently yield less oil per animal — than whales in the Antarctic feeding grounds where most factory ships operate. In addition, whales bear their calves in warmer waters, and land-based whaling crews, therefore, catch more pregnant females and females with calves than pelagic whalers.

The differences between pelagic and land-based whaling required specific sets of regulations tailored for each. Among these measures, the 1937 Convention closed certain areas to factory ships and limited the operation of land stations to six continuous months per year. Nevertheless, the differences between pelagic and land-based whaling continued to pose a significant obstacle to effective whaling regulation.

The 1937 Convention foreshadowed many effective steps taken later in the regulation of whaling. The signatory nations set a partial agenda for future treaties by acknowledging the need to cut the number of whaling vessels further; to provide sanctuaries where whales might "escape molestation"; and to regulate killing methods in order "to abate something of the undoubted cruelty of present methods of whaling." Charactersitcally, whaling-industry opposition slowed the adoption of measures to meet these goals. It took over 40 years to achieve them.

The slightly more restrictive provisions of the 1937 agreement posed two more immediate problems. One was the possibility that nations would try to bypass regulations they had agreed to obey by sending out ships under so-called flags of convenience — that is, their own vessels registered in non-participating nations. Another problem was the danger that some whaling nations would reject the Convention entirely. Such a policy would undermine the effectiveness of any agreement and give renegade countries a competitive advantage over signatory and cooperating nations. In fact, Japan did just that. Its unrestricted whaling effort virtually nullified the 1937 regulations, as nations scrambled to compete for whales while they lasted.

The signatory nations at Washington agreed to meet annually to review data on the previous year's whaling and to modify or extend the regulations as needed. This reflected their belief that regulations were necessary to "the maintenance of the stock of whales and to the prosperity of the whaling industry." These contradictory goals of conservation and economic development defined the fundamental conflict

> "...the 1937 Convention distinguished between pelagic or factory-ship whaling and coastal whaling. Because factory ships can pursue whales anywhere, pelagic whaling deprives whales of any refuge..."

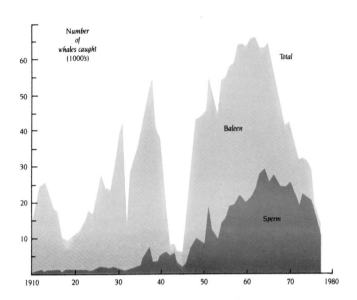

Total annual catches of baleen and sperm whales in all oceans, 1910-1977.

Total Annual Catches of Baleen and Sperm Whales, All Oceans, 1910-1977.

The resumption of whaling following relative inactivity during World War II quickly returned takes to prewar levels. The steep drop that begins in the late 1960s did not result from reduced quotas but from dwindling stocks. During the 1960s, catches consistently fell short of quotas, even though allowable take levels were lowered each year. (After K.R. Allen, 1979)

that was to arise repeatedly in annual meetings under this and later conventions. Unfortunately, economics almost invariably prevailed over conservation, and the tragedy of the commons was enacted yearly by diplomats seeking higher profits for their nation's whaling interests.

World War II was a curse to humankind but a blessing to whales. Whaling vessels were diverted to military duty, and many of them were sunk. Although this gave whales a brief respite from the hunt, naval warfare made the oceans a less-than-tranquil habitat, with exploding depth charges, artillery barrages, and oil spills from sinking tankers. Whales were occasionally mistaken for submarines and killed by bombs.

Mindful of the profits from unrestricted prewar whaling, Antarctic whaling companies were tantalized by prospective recovery of decimated stocks when the war ended. Japan used postwar reconstruction aid from the United States to finance a new whaling fleet that took advantage of technology developed for military purposes during the war. Its factory ships were equipped with sonar to locate submerged whales and radios to coordinate the movement of catcher boats. Other whaling nations converted military ships to whaling vessels and added larger factory ships and faster catcher boats. The hunt recommenced with greater efficiency.

With resumption of whaling came a new attempt at regulation. In December 1946, fourteen whaling nations signed a new International Convention for the Regulation of Whaling. Signatory nations included Argentina, Australia, Brazil, Canada, Chile, Denmark, France, the Netherlands, New Zealand, Norway, Peru, USSR, UK, and USA. Neither Japan nor Germany, due to their status after the War, was initially invited to join. The Convention built upon its predecessors, the 1931 and 1937 Conventions, and established the International Whaling Commission (IWC) to formulate regulations and oversee their implementation on an annual basis.

Despite certain weaknesses, the Convention developed important precedents for international resource management. Firsthand involvement in the previous negotiations gave Remington Kellogg of the United States and Birger Bergerson of Norway — primary authors of the 1946 pact — a knowledge of the failures and successes of previous regulatory efforts. Major weaknesses had been a lack of basic principles on which to base management decisions and the absence of a supervisory body to make those decisions.

Kellogg and Bergerson, therefore, began the 1946 convention document with a set of basic principles. They recognized "the interest of the nations of the world in safeguarding for future generations the great natural resources represented by the whale stocks." They admitted that "the history of whaling has seen overfishing of one area after another and of one species of whale after another to such a degree that it is essential to protect all species of whales from further overfishing." All of this demonstrated the need for conservation, which the convention established as its primary goal.

Yet, Kellogg and Bergerson did not oppose whaling. They argued, instead, that conservation actually supported whaling, noting that "increases in the size of whale stocks will permit increases in the number of whales which may be captured without endangering these natural resources." They specifically hoped to avoid practices that would produce "widespread economic and nutritional distress." This established economic development as the second, equally important principle. The Convention's dual purpose was "the proper conservation of whale stocks and . . . the orderly development of the whaling industry."

The 1946 Convention was the first international agreement for the management of a common resource to declare conservation a primary goal. Previous agreements had focused exclusively on economics and, in the case of fisheries, the division of resources among competing nations. The 1946 Convention also took into account future generations rather than concentrating solely on the present, and on whaling interests in particular.

Despite these advances, the Convention repeated the mistake that had plagued the previous understandings, namely, the refusal to declare which of its two contradictory goals — conservation and economics — was more important. At the time, negotiators thought that any conflicts this ambiguity caused could be resolved by rational people acting in a responsible manner. Events quickly disproved their assumption.

Kellogg and Bergerson expected regulatory disputes to arise, and they outlined a plan for a body that would meet yearly to settle them. Today, under the agreement, the International Whaling Commission meets each summer, usually in the United Kingdom, where it is headquartered. Each signatory nation is represented by a Commissioner who casts one vote when the Commission formulates policy. Regulations are listed on the "Schedule," which can only be amended with the approval of three-quarters of the Commissioners. This requirement makes it difficult to alter the Schedule (either to establish a new regulation or change an existing one), but it also ensures that regulations have widespread support among the Commission members.

Despite the three-quarters majority rule, Kellogg foresaw the possibility that a member nation would find a given regulation so objectionable that it would withdraw from the Convention to avoid compliance. He, therefore, included a provision that allows a nation to exempt itself from any particular amendment to the Schedule by registering an objection to it. Some critics have called this provision a loophole that enables member nations to evade regulations. But

International agreements were formed to manage whale stocks, but "economics almost invariably prevailed over conservation and the tragedy of the commons was enacted yearly by diplomats seeking higher profits for their nation's whaling interests."

Kellogg felt the IWC could not survive without such an escape clause. He believed the Commission would disintegrate if nations fell to bickering over regulations and that its survival was more important than the uniform application of any single rule. The Commission's existence today is due partly to Kellogg's insight.

Because both Kellogg and Bergerson had scientific training, they stipulated that amendments to the Schedule "be based on scientific findings." Again, however, the Convention formalized its basic contradiction with a requirement that in making such decisions, the Commission "take into consideration the interest of the consumers of whale products and the whaling industry."

For the first 25 years of its existence, the IWC presided over the depletion of most great whale stocks and the near extermination of some species. Some critics attribute the Commission's failure to prevent overexploitation to weaknesses in the founding agreement. Others blame Commission members for refusing to act in the face of indisputable evidence of stock depletions. A few have even blamed the Commission's scientific advisors. There is agreement on one point: the fact that an eagerness to protect the economic interests of the whaling industry — and not whales — has lain at the heart of the problem.

The IWC's few defenders assert that it has regulated whaling as effectively as most international fisheries agreements have controlled fishing. Although there is much truth in this argument, it has been widely rejected on the grounds that no amount of problems with other agreements can excuse the IWC's failure to act responsibly. IWC supporters also claim that critics work with the advantage of hindsight and that the issues are never as clear at the time they emerge as they are in retrospect. They argue that the Commission has always used scientific uncertainty about the status of whale stocks as an excuse for regulatory decisions that favor the whaling industry.

Beyond the Article V provision for self-exemption from "objectionable" regulations, critics have pointed to three other weaknesses in the Convention. One is a lack of enforcement power. As in the 1937 agreement, the Commission sets regulations, but responsibility for enforcing them falls to individual nations, which must monitor their own citizens and all vessels registered under their flags. Needless to say, some nations have been less than diligent in this area.

A second weakness is the absence of any provision for limiting the total number of whaling vessels, generally referred to as the "whaling effort." In the years immediately following World War II, nations expanded their whaling fleets to take advantage of the slight recovery of whale stocks that had occurred during the War. As this intensified whaling effort began to deplete stocks once again, the IWC's scientific advisors recommended that quotas be reduced.

Whaling nations, however, worked in concert to raise quotas, hoping to keep their large fleets busy and to maintain the high profits of prewar years. Here again was the conflict between conservation and economic interests that Convention negotiators had hoped could be worked out amicably. A limit on total effort would have strengthened considerably the Commission's conservation role and might have led to quota reductions in time to prevent the depletion of stocks that took place in the 1950s and 1960s.

Finally, the convention did not require the IWC to divide the total quota (number of whales that can be killed in any year) among whaling nations. Though whaling nations met informally to divide the quota, these *ad hoc* meetings were more a source of conflict than cooperation.

These structural shortcomings guaranteed that, by default, economic values would guide the IWC in its decisions on conservation matters. Further, regulations were likely to be weakly enforced; whaling nations were encouraged to lobby for high quotas; and competition among whalers was not discouraged, with increasing numbers of vessels pursuing shrinking stocks. There were no mechanisms designed to strengthen any tendency toward conservation within the IWC or its member nations. Pressure for that position could only be expected to come from outside the Commission structure. It eventually did come from people who opposed depletion of whale stocks for noneconomic reasons. But their concerns about long-term yield were outweighed, at least initially, by the whaling industry's interest in short-term profits.

The International Whaling Commission thus assumed responsibility for conserving whale stocks and regulating whaling under a Convention with a *de facto* bias against both activities. At its first annual meeting in 1949, the IWC asked its newly-formed Scientific and Technical Committee to recommend regulatory measures based on scientific findings. The Commissioners then proceeded to establish regulations and quotas based on the needs of the whaling industry, completely ignoring the Committee proposals. Agreement was reached on size limits, seasons, and closed areas, but these measures where designed primarily to maintain industry profits. Despite a recommendation to the contrary from the Scientific Committee, the Commission replaced the total ban on killing humpback whales in the Antarctic with a generous quota of 1250 whales. It also established a quota of 16,000 Blue Whale units (BWu) for the Antarctic.

The BWu was a gross measure based on the size of different species. With the Blue Whale unit, the Commission sidestepped the issue of setting quotas by species or by stock, a convenience for the whaling industry. Following the Commission meeting, the whaling nations met informally to divide the BWu's among themselves. Whaling fleets then killed whales without regard to species until they filled their BWu quotas.

The 1949 Commission meeting also brought the first objection under Article V, the escape clause "loophole." The Commission had voted to consider as land stations factory ships that operated exclusively within a nation's territorial waters. By restricting the use of these ships, the Commission hoped to maintain the distinction between pelagic and coastal whaling that had proved so troublesome. But an objection filed by France exempted its "coastal" factory ships from the limitation.

The 1949-50 whaling season brought the first quota violations. Whaling nations took 16,059 BWu's (59 over the quota) and exceeded the ceiling on scarce humpbacks by 867, or 70%. The Commission took no action on these violations, passing them off as the unintentional result of poor communication among whaling vessels.

In its first year, then, the IWC set a pattern of failure that continued for the next 20. Scientific advisors recommended lower quotas and other conservation measures; the Commissioners ignored the scientists and set quotas tailored to whaling industry needs. A member nation, fearing that a specific regulation might cost its industry money, filed for an exemption. Other nations followed suit, and a regulation was rendered ineffective at the start. Even where there were no formal objections, many nations evaded the regulations, and the Commission could do little to stop such infractions.

When the Commission did act responsibly, some whaling nations withdrew in protest. Bickering among Antarctic whaling nations during the informal negotiations over the allocation of Blue Whale units led to further withdrawals from the Commission, so, to lure whaling nations back into the Commission, regulations were relaxed even more.

Throughout its initial years, nearly every conservation measure was either

> "**T**he International Whaling Commission . . . assumed responsibility for conserving whale stocks and regulating whaling under a Convention with a **de facto** bias against both activities."

The International Convention for the Regulation of Whaling opened in Washington, November 1946. Fourteen nations signed an agreement establishing the IWC the following month. (Smithsonian Institution photo)

evaded, rescinded or ignored by the IWC and its members. The Commission's capitulation on a range of conservation questions amounted to a declaration of open season on whales during the 1950's and 1960's. As a result, every whale stock declined rapidly.

The larger species — blues, finbacks, rights, sperms, and humpbacks — were killed first. As they were depleted, the smaller species — sei, Bryde's, and Minke whales — became targets as well. Indeed, one way to gauge the decline of the great whales stocks is by tracing the growth in the number of smaller species killed over time. The annual catch of sei whales, for example, increased from under 1,000 in the 1955-56 whaling season to a peak of over 20,000 in 1965-66. In the same period, the annual catch of blue whales plummeted from about 27,000 to 3,000. The catch of minkes showed a similar, but smaller, rise in the early 1970's.

The decline of whale stocks during the first 25 years of IWC regulation can also be seen in the size of whales killed. Under the Blue Whale unit system, whalers preferred to kill the largest whales of any species to fill their quotas, since a 24-m blue brought more profit that an 18-m specimen (80 ft *vs* 60 ft), yet either counted as one BWu. Stock depletion was thus paralleled by a decline in the average size of whales killed. Both the size and number of blue whales killed fell dramatically from the start of postwar whaling to 1965. The size of sperm whales taken in the Arctic showed a similar decrease that began even before World War II.

Every year scientists presented evidence of overexploitation to the Commission and recommended conservation measures. They warned that without quotas, stocks would drop so low that the industry would become unprofitable. But whenever the Commission questioned the Scientific Committee on this subject, the scientists were forced to admit that they could not produce indisputable population figures for whale stocks, nor could they recommend a precise take figure above which whaling would deplete the stocks.

The nations favoring conservation and their scientists interpreted this uncertainty as a strong rationale for lower quotas, arguing that a conservative approach was safest until more definite data were available. The whaling nations and their scientists argued that scientific uncertainty justified higher quotas to meet the industry's economic needs. In the end, the Commission usually ignored the scientists' warnings and voted for quotas high enough to maintain industry profits in the short-term, even if it was detrimental to industry profits in the long-term. From the whalers' point of view, there was more money to be made by killing as many whales as possible, as quickly as possible, and investing the profits in other enterprises, than there was in conserving whale stocks for the future.

In 1963 the scientists' predictions were finally confirmed. Against the Scientific Committee's recommendations for lower limits, the Commission had enacted an Antarctic quota of 10,000 Blue Whale units, but the whaling industry's best efforts yielded only 8429 BWu's. Even though the whaling nations now admitted that the stocks were depleted, they still continued to oppose conservation measures. In 1964, the Scientific Committee pressed the Commission to replace the blue-whale unit system with a system of quotas for individual species. The Commission again ignored its own advisors and adopted a quota of 8000 Blue Whale units; fewer than 7000 were caught.

This trend continued for several years, with the Commission rejecting the Scientific Committee's recommendations and setting quotas the industry was unable to fill. The scientists knew that some species were approaching extinction and recommended total protection for blue, right, and humpback whales; the Commission refused to follow their advice. The Commission also ignored a recommendation that sanctuaries be established in certain areas to protect the few remaining whales.

By 1970 there was no longer any question of preventing the depletion of stocks and decline of the industry. The only question was how the dying industry might be prevented from exterminating entire species. In the elegant conference halls of London, few Commissioners of the whaling nations had demonstrated any understanding of the problem, much less a willingness to help. Most of them conducted both fisheries and whaling negotiations for their countries, and many saw no difference between the two. As a group they were sensitive not to the biology of whales but rather to the economics of whaling.

A few Commissioners and scientific advisors had grown increasingly frustrated with this refusal to promote conservation. They had repeatedly advanced conservation plans based on concrete findings about population and reproductive rates. In debates before the Commission, the whaling nations had generally responded to these proposals with unsubstantiated data and arguments that seemed illogical to most observers. Yet, in a string of decisions reached during the mid- and late 1960s, the IWC consistently favored positions backed by the whaling interests. By 1970, the dissenting Commissioners and scientists had decided on a new tactic, an appeal to the public for support of a stronger conservation program.

"By 1970 there was no longer any question of preventing the depletion of stocks and decline of the industry. The only question was how the dying industry might be prevented from exterminating entire species."

The Struggle for Protection

In the early 1970's, the whaling situation captured the American imagination. In books, films, music, television, and other media, the wonder and tragedy of whales were presented to the public. Conservation scientists presented the scientific point of view in scholarly as well as popular articles and books. Artists working in many media devoted their talents to the cause. Politicians hopped on the bandwagon and propounded the need to protect whales. Environmentalists lobbied in Congress for legislation to protect whales and persuaded President Richard Nixon and his Interior Secretary, Walter Hickel, to promote conservation in the selection of the American delegation to the IWC. With few American interests at stake, this was a safe enough position for the administration to adopt.

The atmosphere for this public campaign could not have been more receptive. The American people were rediscovering their maritime tradition and the value of marine resources through Jacques Cousteau's and other television programs. A growing concern with educational problems, grouped under the catch phrase "why Johnny can't read," centered on communication. With many critics blaming television for declining communication skills among young people, the notion that whales can communicate suggested that there might be more to this issue than electronics.

A more significant influence was the rapidly growing environmental movement. The first Earth Day, in April 1970, provoked a surge of public support for conservation and environmental protection. The scope of environmental problems was dismaying: forests were being clear-cut by timber companies; air and fresh water were being polluted by every imaginable enterprise with little concern for public health; and food was being laced heavily with chemical agents designed to retard spoilage and "enhance" flavor. The whaling controversy became another of the stones in the mosaic of environmental destruction. But to many people, whales carried a special significance because they provided a focus, a point at which so many of the other problems overlapped.

Early in 1972, a lobbying campaign waged by the environmental movement culminated in passage of the *Marine Mammal Protection Act* by the U.S. Congress. A coalition of animal rights, anti-cruelty, and environmental professionals had joined with conservationists and scientists to formulate the precedent-setting Act. For the first time, the conservation of a resource was declared to be more important than its economic value. The Act imposed a moratorium on the killing of all marine mammals within U.S. jurisdiction but provided exemptions for certain aboriginal peoples dependent on marine mammals for subsistence purposes. The Act also called for the elimination of incidental taking of marine mammals — that is, killing or injuring them in the course of commercial fishing or other activities. This provision proved especially troublesome to tuna fishermen, whose purse seine nets were trapping and killing hundreds of thousands of porpoises each year. The Act prohibited the harassment of marine mammals, a provision that forced whale-watchers to take special care in their observation of animals and prevented fishermen from shooting at seals they suspected of eating their fish or damaging their nets. Finally, the Act established the Marine Mammal Commission as an independent body to make policy recommendations at the Federal level based on sound scientific evidence.

The whale also emerged as the primary symbol of the international environmental movement in 1972. At the United Nations Conference on the Human Environment in Stockholm, developed and developing nations found it difficult to agree on the fundamental problems of pollution and habitat

> "...the destruction of an entire order of highly evolved, intelligent, gentle beings is not trivial. The whales can be saved — and in saving them we can create a model of international action that can demonstrate a way to save ourselves and the rest of the earth we cherish."
>
> Joan McIntyre

The environmental movement in the early 1970s moved environmental issues — including whale protection — into the political mainstream of countries around the world.

(Chip Berlet photo, courtesy The Population Institute)

destruction. Less-developed nations attacked the concern for environmental quality espoused by developed nations as a luxury they could not afford. They perceived two overriding needs for themselves — increased agricultural production and the most rapid industrialization possible. They saw environmentalism as an industrial-nation ploy intended to maintain former colonies as dependent suppliers of raw material. In this context of angry suspicion, the overexploitation of whales surfaced as an issue upon which all but Japan could agree. The Conference unanimously passed a call for a ten-year moratorium on all commercial whaling. Japan abstained.

The United States carried the moratorium resolution from Stockholm to the IWC meeting in London and proposed that the Commission endorse it. Supporters of the moratorium proposal argued that overfished whale stocks could not recover without it. The Commission turned to the Scientific Committee for advice on the proposal. The Committee judged the moratorium to be without scientific foundation and reported that it preferred a program of responsible management that treated stocks individually (sperm whales in the North Pacific, for example, or humpbacks in the North Atlantic). The Committee could not accept a blanket moratorium on all commercial whaling as a scientifically valid method for managing whale resources. Ironically, in view of its record of ignoring the Scientific Committee, the full Commission accepted the recommendation to reject the moratorium proposal.

Though defeated, the moratorium proposal had substantial effect on the Commission. Prior to 1972, the Commission had been split into two factions — the whaling nations, which argued for high quotas and few regulations, and the conservation nations, which argued for scientific management on a stock-by-stock basis. In most cases, the whaling bloc had prevailed over the conservationist group. As one example, scientists had been working to persuade the Commission to abandon the Blue Whale unit since 1963, but the Commission had resisted the move because it would cause difficulties for the whaling industry and eventually lead to lower quotas. The introduction of the moratorium proposal suddenly transformed the "extreme" BWu revision position into a moderate stance. Now the Commission was confronted with three alternatives: the high quotas favored by whaling nations, the Scientific Committee's recommendations, or a ten-year moratorium on all whaling. Compromises were struck in order to gain the three-quarters majority required for actions, and the new middle position — the Scientific Committee recommendations — emerged as the ultimate choice of the Commission.

In 1974, the Commission formally adopted an Australian proposal for a "New Management Procedure" as a compromise between the moratorium and the whaling nations' position. The Blue Whale unit was abolished, and the Scientific Committee began recommending quotas on a stock-by-stock basis. This marked the beginning of responsible resource management by the IWC.

The New Management Procedure (NMP) is based on the concept of maximum sustainable yield (MSY). Stocks that are below MSY are considered depleted and receive a "Protected" classification. Stocks that are at or above MSY are classified as "Sustained Management," and quotas are set at levels designed to maintain the stocks. If there are no data on population, but the stock is thought to be at or above MSY, it is classified as "Initial Management," and a quota may be set for it, too.

There are several problems with MSY and the New Management Procedure. One is lack of sufficient population data for many stocks. Most data come from whaling vessels and are based on catch per unit effort (CPUE) — like MSY, a concept borrowed from fisheries management. CPUE assumes that the number of whales killed in a given period of time reflects the total number of whales in the stock. If the population is small, whaling crews will spend more time hunting whales and, therefore, catch fewer per day than if there are many around.

CPUE is a good theoretical measure of stock abundance, but it has flaws, not the least of them the fact that the data come from the whaling industry, which has much to gain from inflating its figures. Another problem with CPUE is the likelihood that increases in technological efficiency will reduce effort, even when stocks decline. In this way, a constant CPUE might mask a shrinking stock. Finally, when good CPUE data are available, MSY is still difficult to calculate. Although modern commercial whaling began nearly 100 years ago, reliable records were not kept until the 1920's. This has magnified the difficulty of determining the maximum population size for any stock. Scientists are forced to use complex mathematical models based on data from recent years to "reconstruct" stock populations. As in any application of mathematical models, whenever there are questions about the validity of data, scientists disagree about the models' results.

The difficulties in calculating MSY sparked disagreement in the Scientific Committee — ironically, at just the time the IWC began to heed its recommendations. The Committee does not vote on its recommendations to the Commission; it operates by consensus. Furthermore, Committee members do not represent their respective countries, but rather attempt to act as individuals whose only loyalty is to the standards of their profession.

Disagreements over the classification of stocks and appropriate quota levels under the NMP, therefore, presented a problem: should the Committee make no recommendation if it could not reach consensus on an issue, or should formal votes be taken? The first course would have been irresponsible, especially after the long campaign to convince the Commission to follow Committee advice. The latter course would have violated a long-standing tradition and probably would have politicized the Committee.

The Committee chose a classic third course: equivocation. Rather than presenting the Commission with one recommendation, the Committee began offering multiple recommendations in cases where there was substantial disagreement. The Scientific Committee reports began to include the language of qualification: "most members think" this, while "many think" that, "others think" this, and "some think" that. This equivocation left the final decision to the Commission, yet it established the boundaries within which the Commission should act.

In effect, the initial moratorium proposal finally vested in the Scientific Committee the power that Kellogg and Bergerson, authors of the Convention, had intended it to have. The Scientific Committee now would initiate the decision-making process by analyzing the data and then make recommendations to the Commission. Though not legally bound, the Commissioners were morally obligated to act within the bounds of the recommendations.

The scope of the political struggle between whaling and conservation nations narrowed. The whaling nations lobbied for the highest recommended quotas and least restrictive regulations, and the conservation countries for the lowest and most restrictive. To achieve a three-quarters vote required compromise, and the resulting IWC action usually did not represent a threat to the whale stocks.

Having initiated the moratorium proposal, the United States became the leading proponent of the Scientific Committee's most conservative recommendations within

Thomas B. Grooms, Executive Director of the Center for Environmental Education, visited the Pribilof Islands in the Bering Sea as a part of the Center's marine mammal protection efforts. The Bering Sea is one of the most productive marine ecosystems in the world and is the primary feeding ground for certain stocks of humpback, bowhead and gray whales. (Pamela Williams Photo)

the IWC. Its scientists and Commissioner argued that scientific uncertainty over the status of whale stocks dictated that the most restrictive methods be adopted to avoid depleting stocks out of ignorance as well as greed. The debates were bitter, but some conservative recommendations passed. Smaller whaling nations were persuaded to abandon Japan and the Soviet Union and to vote with the conservationist countries — though not without difficulty. "If we should submit ourselves completely to the Scientific Committee," remarked Commission Chairman Rindahl of Norway (now one of the small whaling nations), "it might be too much of a good thing." Nevertheless, in 1976, the Commission accepted all but one of the Scientific Committee's recommendations.

The United States was influential in the IWC for a number of reasons. First, it was the undisputed world leader in conservation and environmental protection. Its system of national parks, forests, and wilderness areas was testimony to its conservation policies. The National Environmental Policy Act (NEPA) and the Environmental Protection Agency that it established were considered innovative elements of a responsible national policy that many nations hoped to emulate. The nation's economic power and political influence also contributed.

A most powerful U.S. tool at the IWC bargaining table is a law called the Pelly Amendment. It allows the President of the U.S. to embargo fisheries products from any nation that undermines the effectiveness of an international agreement or organization. Since the U.S. is a major market for fisheries products from many whaling nations, it is able to persuade those nations to support conservationist positions within the IWC and to forego exempting themselves under Article V. Against Japan's and the Soviet Union's desire to escape IWC restrictions, the Pelly Amendment is particularly effective.

In 1977 the United States reached the height of its influence in the IWC. Using sophisticated computer models, the Scientific Committee produced very conservative recommendations for the Commission. The U.S. assembled coalitions in support of conservation, and quotas were reduced an impressive 36% from the previous year. The Scientific Committee, however, also recommended that the U.S. stop the killing of bowhead whales by Alaskan Eskimos, a recommendation that led to the decline of U.S. leadership in the IWC.

In the case of the Alaskan bowhead hunt, the dark past of Yankee whaling — the killing of calves to capture their mothers and the wholesale slaughter of whales for corset stays and oil — returned to haunt the U.S. Between 1848 and 1920, over 20,000 bowhead whales had been killed, primarily by American whaling crews. This left the North Pacific stock on the edge of extinction, yet Alaskan natives continued to hunt them. Unlike commercial whalers, the Eskimos used the entire whale. They ate the meat and blubber and used other parts for a variety of subsistence needs. The hunt itself was a ritual in which villages renewed their kinship ties by distributing the meat and blubber among related villages. It was a ritual as sacred to the Eskimos as holy communion is to some Christians.

The Scientific Committee, however, limited its considerations to scientific matters. The Committee expressed its concern over the low level of the bowhead population and asked the U.S. to conduct research that would determine more precisely the size of the stock and the number of whales being killed each year by the Eskimos. The Committee was troubled particularly by reports that Eskimos were using motor boats and high-powered rifles to kill bowheads, and that they were striking and fatally wounding but losing many more whales than they were landing. But the U.S. government was reluctant to follow the Scientific Committee's recommendation that the hunt be stopped. It hesitated to undertake the requested research for fear that it would upset relations with Eskimos. It thus found itself lobbying against IWC acceptance of the Scientific Committee's most conservative recommendation on the issue, after working nearly two decades to persuade the Commission to follow such advice.

In 1978, the U.S. effectively joined the ranks of the whaling nations. Its research program indicated that bowheads were indeed on the edge of extinction, and that any kills whatsoever would endanger the stock. The Scientific Committee recommended a total ban on killing bowhead whales. The U.S., however, requested a modest quota to fulfill the needs of the Eskimos, and used the influence it had previously employed for conservation to get the quota passed by the Commission. Without American influence, nonwhaling nations were unable to secure many of the conservation measures recommended by the Scientific Committee.

In addition to the loss of U.S. leadership, the bowhead issue altered the decision-making process of the IWC. Prior to this episode, the process had been simple: the Scientific Committee made recommendations and the full Commission acted on them. There was also a Technical Committee, a body without formal responsibility that actually consisted of the Commissioners acting as a committee-of-the-whole. Because passage of motions in the Technical Committee only required a simple majority of votes, Commissioners used the Committee to determine whether controversial measures could attract the three-quarters majority needed for passage of final actions in plenary session. The U.S. had discovered the value of the Technical Committee while lobbying for the bowhead quota and successfully campaigned for its formal establishment as an intermediary between the Scientific Committee and the Commission Plenary. This has weakened the influence of the Scientific Committee by making it easier for the Commission to

Anti-whaling demonstration, Kyoto, Japan, 1978. (John Perry photo)

73

Demonstrators at Brighton, England, during International Whaling Commission meeting, 1980. Ashes in foreground are from flags of whaling nations which were burned earlier. (John J Domont photo)

ignore the scientists' recommendations. The Commission now can choose to accept the proposals of either committee and claim publicly to be following the recommendations of an advisory group. The fact that the Technical Committee is neither a scientific nor an advisory body — it is the full Commission acting under a different name and set of rules — is conveniently overlooked.

Following the victory on bowhead quotas, the U.S. resumed its pressure for a moratorium on commercial whaling, using an argument reformulated to accommodate its bowhead position. The U.S. began to argue that scientific uncertainty over the status of whale stocks made responsible management impossible, and that a moratorium was the only way to ensure against depleting whale resources. Nevertheless, it had sacrificed much of its effectiveness as a leader on conservation issues, and other nonwhaling nations took up the cause.

In 1979, the Commission designated the Indian Ocean a whale sanctuary and passed a limited moratorium on pelagic whaling — with an exception for Minke whales. Some members of the Scientific Committee supported the measure on grounds that pelagic whaling deprived whales of any refuge, an issue that had been raised over 40 years earlier at both Geneva and Washington. Other scientists agreed that uncertainty over the status of many stocks justified a moratorium, marking a notable shift in the use of the uncertainty argument from a whaling-nation excuse for high quotas to a conservationist argument for a moratorium.

The IWC had finally begun to fulfill its conservation goal. In 1980, however, the bowhead issue again stymied attempts at quota reductions. A temporary solution, in the form of a three-year bowhead quota, allowed the U.S. to resume its conservation efforts.

The Future

The future is uncertain for whales, for whaling, for the IWC and the whale protection movement. Some stocks have been so badly depleted that they may never recover, and even if whaling ceases, there will be other obstacles to recovery. Commercial fishing is rapidly depleting many of the world's fish stocks and, in the process, reducing the capacity of the marine habitat to support whales. Soon the primary food of baleen whales in the Antarctic, the tiny, shrimplike krill, will be harvested on a vast scale for human use. Human competition for food will complicate the recovery of the great whale stocks.

The whaling industry seems to be dying. Reduced quotas and increasing fuel costs have eaten into profits. The fleets built in the 1950's boom are aging, but companies hesitate to replace them in view of falling returns. Aboriginal whaling will probably continue unless or until stocks are exterminated.

The IWC's fate is also difficult to predict. Several nonwhaling nations have joined the Commission in order to promote whale conservation, and others may follow. This will increase the chances of passing a complete moratorium, but it also may so perturb whaling nations that they simply abandon the Commission. This has happened before, and if it does again, nonwhaling nations may be forced once again to relax regulations in order to bring whaling nations back into the Commission.

The whale protection movement faces difficult challenges, and the most important of them may be its own success. Many people think that whales have been saved from the direct threat of whaling and are now turning their attention to the indirect threat of habitat destruction. Though safeguarding marine habitat is important to the survival and recovery of whales, as an issue it lacks the broad appeal of whales themselves. The forces involved — commercial fishing, offshore oil development, and ocean dumping of toxic wastes — are not as fundamentally repulsive as whaling, and the United States is, in this area, just as guilty of destructive activities as Japan and the Soviet Union. To survive, the whale protection movement will need to widen its focus to include issues like habitat protection that affect both humans and whales, and it will need to educate and mobilize the public on these issues without relaxing the pressure against whaling.

The **Center for Environmental Education** was formed in 1972 as a private, non-profit organization to increase public awareness and understanding of the relationship between ourselves and our planet. In response to growing human population and demand for marine resources, the Center has become a leading advocate for the protection of the oceans and their wealth of life including whales, seals and sea turtles. More than 440,000 sponsors support us in the fight to maintain biological diversity and the ecosystem integrity of the seas.

For further information about the programs of the Center for Environmental Education and how you can get involved, write: Information, **Center for Environmental Education,** 624 9th Street, N.W. Washington, DC 20001.

Call to Action

If recent action in the IWC has saved whales from extinction, it is only because those concerned about whales made themselves heard. They alerted the public to the whales' plight through books and articles, films and television shows, music and the visual arts, and direct mail appeals. The public responded to this human voice of the whale with letters and petitions, telephone calls and telegrams, protests and rallies, and financial contributions to the cause. It took time — and the struggle is not over — but the movement was successful in setting the IWC on a course of conservation.

The United States led the fight for this change in IWC thinking but has recently retreated from its leadership role. When the Scientific Committee recommended an end to the hunting of bowhead whales in 1978, the U.S. abandoned its commitment to following the Committee's most conservative recommendations and began protecting its own interest like any other whaling nation. It will take public action to get the U.S. back on course in the IWC.

United States leadership in the IWC reflected its world leadership in the environmental movement. America has one of the cleaner and safer environments in the industrial world. Other nations have used its environmental laws and regulations as models for their own policies. As this book goes to press, the United States is abandoning its position as an environmental leader in much the same way that it gave up its role in the IWC.

Now is the time to be heard. Use whatever medium you like to let policy-makers know where you stand on whale protection and other environmental issues. The world cannot afford to lose U.S. leadership in these areas. Unless we make ourselves heard, the human voice of nature will sing alone in a ruined world, and we will have ourselves to blame.

Stay Informed

If you are concerned about whales and other environmental issues, you need to stay informed. Newspapers, television, and general interest magazines sometimes provide useful information on specific issues, but their coverage is inconsistent and lacks detail. Better sources are publications specializing in environmental issues. Armed with the specific information they provide, you can make a much more persuasive case when dealing with government officials or private interests. You will also pick up information by discussing issues with family, friends, and co-workers. For more information, write the Center for Environmental Education, 624 9th Street NW, Washington, D.C. 20001.

Lobby and Vote

Ask candidates for public office what they think about whale protection and related environmental issues. If they avoid specific answers, press them until they tell you precisely where they stand. When those issues come up, remind officeholders by letter or telephone of their promises. Do not hesitate to contact public officials, particularly legislators, several times as an issue progresses; that is no more than a professional lobbyist would do. Challenge them on facts or the logic of their arguments and supply them with new information.

If you approve of legislators' work, let them know in a letter. If you are unhappy with their performance, or you find them unresponsive, let them know that you will vote against them when they next run for office. A more persuasive sanction is to work to unseat them in the next primary and general election.

Tell Your Government What You Want

When an issue comes up, let the appropriate appointed and elected officials know what you think they should do. Send letters or telegrams, or make phone calls; have friends and family do the same. This does work. Government officials do not hear from voters as often as might be expected. As a rule of thumb, they will assume that a phone call from one citizen represents a thousand more who are concerned. A telegram counts for one hundred concerned citizens, and a letter, ten. Letters also force officials to think about an issue enough to formulate a position and respond to you in writing. If the response is unsatisfactory, write to say so. Once you know where an elected official stands you can decide whether to vote for him or her — or, more important, whether to work against that official in the next election.

Local and State Level

Important decisions about whales and other environmental issues are not made solely at the federal level. If an issue is local, call the mayor or appropriate municipal official, and your city or town council representative. You can get their names and numbers from the city or town hall.

Write, cable, or call your governor, state senator, and state representatives about state concerns. Most states have an information service that will supply their addresses and telephone numbers over the phone; Directory Assistance for your state capital will give you the number of your state's information service.

Federal Level

Write, cable, or call the President, cabinet members, senators and representatives. Their addresses and telephone numbers are listed below.

President of the
  United States
The White House
Washington, D.C. 20500
(202) 456-1414

Let the President know what you think on every issue. "Letter counts" can influence executive branch decisions in some instances.

Secretary of State
Department of State
Washington, D.C. 20520
(202) 655-4000

The State Department plays a major role in IWC affairs and oversees U.S. policy pertaining to other, related international issues.

Secretary of Interior
Department of Interior
Washington, D.C. 20240
(202) 343-1100

The Departments of Interior and Commerce establish and enforce regulations that affect whales and other marine mammals.

Secretary of Commerce
Department of Commerce
Washington, D.C. 20230
(202) 377-2000

Administrator
Environmental Protection
  Agency
Washington, D.C. 20460
(202) 655-4000

The EPA Administrator is charged with protecting the environment. Tell her or him what problems concern you and what you want to see done about them.

Low Consumptive (Aquaria)
Direct non-consumptive
Indirect non-consumptive
Low Consumptive (Research)

Estimated value of combined low- and nonconsumptive uses of whales in 1981 (see page 81 for a description of specific categories). These uses totalled over $100 million in 1981; the highest available estimate for the world of commercial whaling is $500 million, and some sources suggest a much lower figure.

The growing value of whales in economic activities other than whaling is a significant trend and provides an important argument for protecting whales.

Your Senator
U.S. Senate
Washington, D.C. 20510
(202) 224-3121

Senators and Representatives enact laws and decide how much of your tax money will be spent on environmental research and protection.

Your Representative
House of Representatives
Washington, D.C. 20515
(202) 224-3121

Local Directory Assistance can provide a tollfree number for the state office of most Senators and Representatives.

Tell Other Nations What You Want

For the protection of global resources like whales, the actions of other national governments are also very important. Almost every nation maintains an embassy in the District of Columbia; Directory Assistance (1-202-555-1212) can provide telephone numbers. Addresses for the primary whaling nations and their supporters in the IWC are listed below. Write to tell them you want the killing of whales stopped.

Embassy of Japan
2520 Massachusetts Avenue NW
Washington, D.C. 20008

Embassy of the USSR
1125 16th Street NW
Washington, D.C. 20003

Embassy of Spain
2700 15th Street NW
Washington, D.C. 20009

Embassy of Iceland
2022 Connecticut Avenue NW
Washington, D.C. 20008

Embassy of Korea
2320 Massachusetts Avenue NW
Washington, D.C. 20008

Embassy of Chile
1732 Massachusetts Avenue NW
Washington, D.C. 20036

Embassy of Peru
1700 Massachusetts Avenue NW
Washington, D.C. 20036

Embassy of Norway
2720 34th Street NW
Washington, D.C. 20008

Embasssy of Brazil
3006 Massachusetts Avenue NW
Washington, D.C. 20008

Rallies and Protests

These venerable forms of political expression have played significant roles in our national history. Organizing a rally for whales or a protest against whaling helps spread the word. A rally for an elected official who voted for whale protection and other environmental legislation can generate valuable publicity that will be much appreciated at election time.

Boycott

In 1973, several whale protection organizations initiated a general boycott of Russian and Japanese products as a protest against commercial whaling. The effect of the boycott has not been determined. Some observers think it has put more pressure on Japan and the Soviet Union; others think it has made the whalers even more resistant to conservation.

Boycotts, however, can be very effective. If you oppose the policies or practices of a corporation or country, you can express your opposition by not buying its products. Organize and publicize your opposition. To increase the effectiveness of a boycott, write the chief executive officer of the firm to explain the reasons for your action. This should cause some concern. If enough people write to express support for the action, the firm's head will probably have the matter looked into. When an organized group of people does it, you can be certain of receiving a response.

Stockholder Resolutions

If you own stock in a corporation, you have, in theory, a say in how the firm is run. That includes corporate environmental policy. Holders of large blocks of stock obviously have more say than small stockholders, but even the single-share owner can be heard.

The rules are complicated, but any stockholder is entitled to submit resolutions for consideration at a corporation's annual meeting. Such resolutions are rarely adopted, but they can lead the corporation to reevaluate or clarify its environmental policies. Even a resolution that alters no policy at least forces other stockholders to think about the issue raised. Such educational benefits are small but important gains. Write the Interfaith Center for Corporate Responsibility (475 Riverside Drive, New York, NY 10027) for *The Shareholder's Manual*, a step-by-step guide to preparing and submitting a stockholder proposal.

Use the Media

Take advantage of opportunities in your community to educate other citizens about issues relating to whales and other environmental concerns. Letters to the editors of local newspapers are a good place to start, and suburban weeklies are particularly open to them. Limit your letter to one or two clear points backed up with facts, and give the interested reader a task such as telephoning or writing a specific elected official or national embassy. Some papers will accept well-written essays for their editorial pages, and most radio stations will allow you to tape a one- to two-minute spot on a given issue, particularly if they have run an editorial on the subject recently. The producers of local public affairs programs on television are often receptive to suggestions for topics. Write to ask whether they have considered whales and the movement to protect them.

A more ambitious project is to prepare a briefing kit for editorial writers and reporters at community newspapers and radio or television stations. Such kits should include information on whales and marine mammals, copies of three or four articles on a specific topic, and directions for further research on the subject (books, articles, local experts willing to be interviewed). In a sense, you are acting as a lobbyist, but particularly in coastal areas where whales can be seen, this background information on a potential story will usually be appreciated.

Send Money

Environmental organizations need money to continue working against whaling and to defend environmental laws and regulations against pressures for relaxation in the name of "increased productivity" and "improved business climate." Send a tax-deductible contribution to the organization of your choice. The Center for Environmental Education (624 9th Street NW, Washington, D.C. 20001) needs your support.

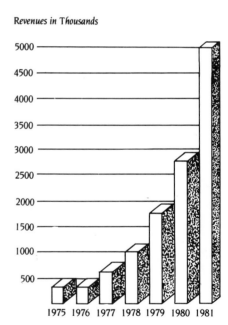

Revenues in Thousands

Growth of Revenues from Whale-Watch Cruises, 1975-81 (East and West Coast Combined)
The growth of interest in whale-watching in recent years has been dramatic. In addition to direct payments to cruise operators, whale-watchers spend money for such related goods and services as lodging, transportation and food.

Field Guide to the Great Whales

Introduction

Watching whales in their natural habitats has become an important recreational activity. In 1976, fewer than 100,000 people went on whale-watching cruises off the Pacific and Atlantic coasts of the United States. In 1981, that number will exceed 500,000, and boat fares will surpass $5 million. When related travel costs and other expenditures by whale-watchers are included, the industry's annual worth reaches $30 million. In addition, 500,000 people will observe whales from strategic land positions in 1981, and they, too, will spend money for travel, food, and related items.

Whale-watching represents a valuable use of whale resources that does not require killing or injuring them; this classifies it as a "direct nonconsumptive" use of whales. There are also indirect nonconsumptive uses of whales, and their value is rising, too. The production and sale of whale representations in books, periodicals, films, television, music, photographs, the fine arts, and other media constitute an indirect use worth at least $20 million annually. In addition to direct and indirect nonconsumptive uses, certain uses of whales are considered low-consumptive because they involve only a few animals. The capture and display of small whale species in oceanariums such as Marine Land and Sea World is a low-consumptive use worth over $50 million yearly. Scientific research is another low-consumptive use.

The total value of these low- and nonconsumptive uses of whales exceeds $100 million a year, about one-fifth the value of commercial whaling. This comparison of uses is insufficient, however, because it does not include the aesthetic and educational value of low-/nonconsumptive uses, which, though difficult to measure in purely monetary terms, is nevertheless significant.

A major question this comparison raises is whether low-/nonconsumptive and consumptive uses are compatible. On one hand, whales that are hunted tend to avoid all ships, including those carrying whale-watchers. Commercial whaling thus reduces the whale-watcher's chances of seeing whales. On the other hand, some people go whale-watching and buy whale books and other representations because they believe the animals are in danger of extinction and thus value them highly, as they do other rare things.

The economic value of living whales is increasing while the value of commercial whaling is decreasing. If a moratorium on whaling is instituted, and whale stocks are allowed to recover and repopulate the world's oceans, the potential value of whaling will begin to increase. At that point humankind would be able to choose whether to resume the hunt. But at least there would be a choice to make.

Virtually "standing" in the water, a spyhopping finback whale studies a whale-watching boat. (Marine Mammal Fund photo)

Blue Whale

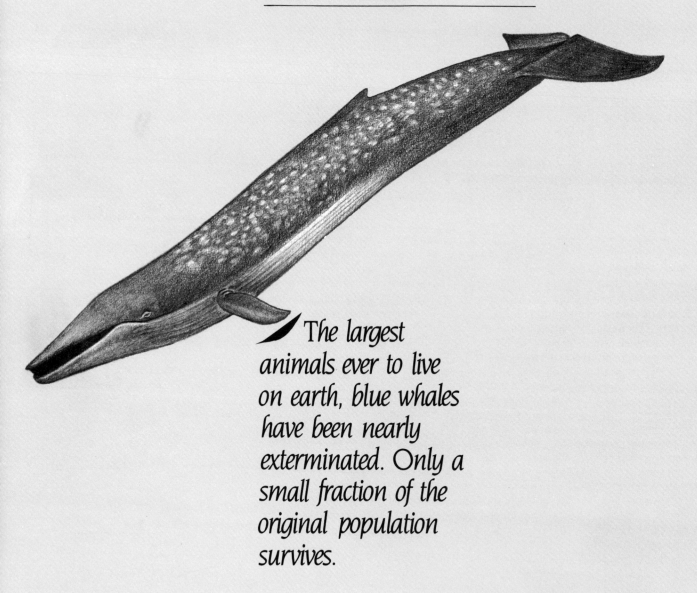

The largest animals ever to live on earth, blue whales have been nearly exterminated. Only a small fraction of the original population survives.

Illustration by Sara Meade

Blue Whale (Balaenoptera musculus)

translation: *"muscle whale"*

Description. Although a blue whale can attain a length of more than 30.5 m (100 ft) and a weight of 118 to 136 metric tons (130-150 tons), most of the largest were killed prior to the beginning of international protection in 1966. Today, most blues sighted range between 21 m and 27 m (70 to 90 ft).

The head of a blue whale is flat and broad with a single ridge extending almost to the tip of the snout. The dorsal fin is about 33 centimeters (13 inches), small in proportion to the whale's size; it grows from the rear third of the whale's back.

The skin of a blue whale is, predictably, a consistent blue/gray color with gray/white mottling. Accumulated diatoms, however, frequently give the belly a yellow cast that inspired one nickname, "sulphur bottom." The flippers are blue-gray on top and light blue on the underside. The flukes, often raised before a deep dive, are the same blue-gray as the rest of the body, and the baleen is black. A blue whale's slender blow can reach 9.1 m (30 ft) in height.

Natural History. Female blues give birth about once every three years following a 12-month pregnancy. The newborn calves measure 6 to 7.6 m (20 to 25 ft) and weigh 2.7 metric tons (3 t) They gain as much as 750 kilograms (200 pounds) a day while nursing on the fat-rich milk of their mothers. Males are considered mature at 5 years, females at 7.

Blue whales feed on krill and stay primarily in cold waters where krill are abundant. Since krill abound in the top 100 meters (300 ft) of water, blues rarely have to dive very far to obtain food.

The distinct swimming behavior of blue whales by itself can serve as a clue for their identification at sea. When moving at low speeds, a blue's blowhole and a portion of its head may be visible once the dorsal fin comes into sight. The whale then settles slowly into the water. When moving quickly, or about to make a deep dive, the head and blowhole disappear, and a great length of the whale's back surfaces and submerges. The small dorsal fin is seen briefly; then the animal lifts its tail flukes out of the water before slipping from sight. The flukes are not lifted as high or as prominently as those of the humpback and sperm whales.

WHAT TO LOOK FOR

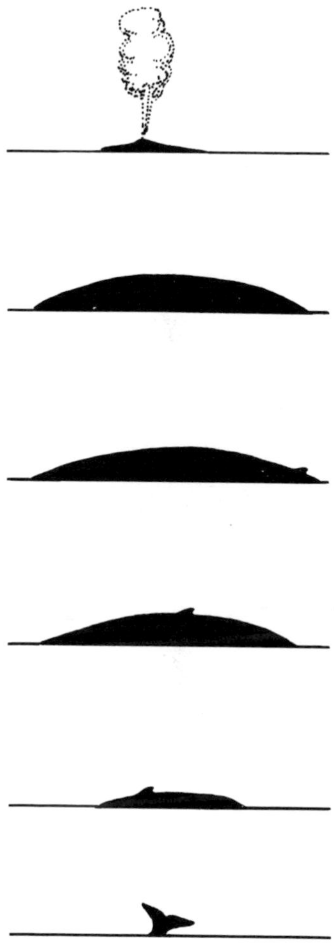

83

Population and Distribution. Worldwide there may be only 6,000 to 10,000 blues; the estimated pre-whaling count was 300,000. They are distributed fairly widely across the Atlantic, Pacific, and Indian Oceans, as well as in the Antarctic and Arctic regions.

Although the movements of blue whales are poorly understood, they are thought to follow well-defined patterns, feeding in cold, biologically productive waters in the summer and moving toward the tropics and warmer seas for the winter.

blue whale

(*Gray area = distribution*)

Bowhead Whale

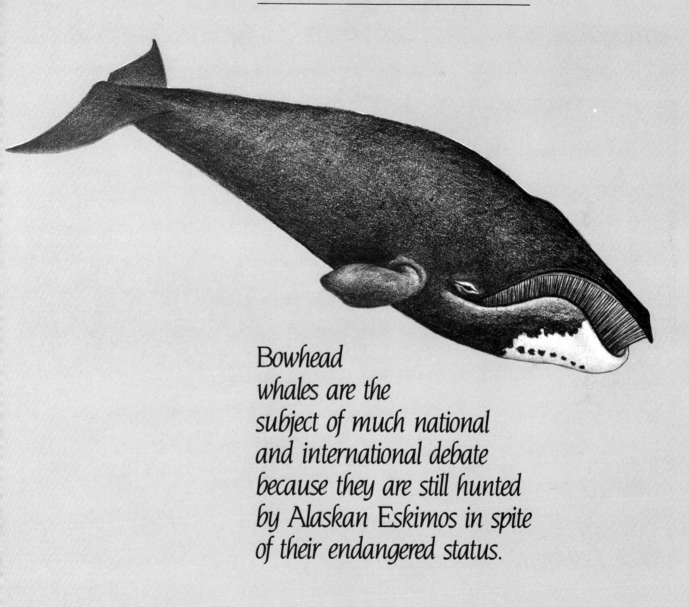

Bowhead whales are the subject of much national and international debate because they are still hunted by Alaskan Eskimos in spite of their endangered status.

Illustration by Sara Meade

Bowhead Whale (Balaena mysticetus)

translation: *"mustache whale"*

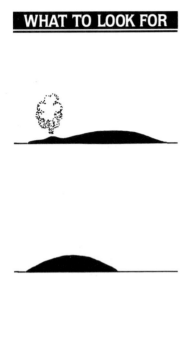

Description. Bowhead whales — the name comes from the exaggerated arch of their jaws and heads — attain lengths of 20 m (65 ft) and may weigh over 50 metric tons (55 t). Another stout species, they move slowly, rarely exceeding 6 knots. A bowhead's baleen, at 4.5 m (14 ft), is the longest of any species. Runner-up honors go to right whales, with 2.1-m (7-ft) baleen.

When viewed while swimming, the backs of some bowheads appear curved. The first curve extends from the snout to a point just behind the blowholes, and a second one runs from the back of the head to the tail. A bowhead's back is completely smooth and lacks a dorsal fin. On the ventral (bottom) side, there are no rorqual grooves.

Bowheads are black except for a white band beneath the chin that looks something like a necklace. Flippers and flukes are black, and the flukes are often raised on a deep dive. The widely spaced blowholes of the bowhead produce a distinctive, 4.5-meter (15-foot), V-shaped blow.

Natural History. Bowheads may be found alone or in small groups. Autumn concentrations of up to 40 are not uncommon as the whales make their way from summer mating grounds to more southerly winter feeding areas. Bowheads feed exclusively on copepods and krill, which they strain from the water with their long, fine baleen. As with right whales, high oil content and the utility of the baleen made bowheads a prize catch in the 19th century.

Bowheads occasionally breach, throwing themselves out of the water and landing with great splashes.

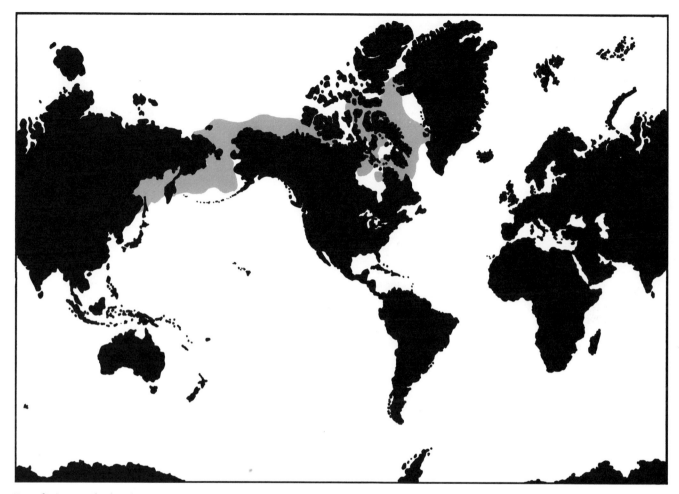

Population and Distribution. Approximately 2100 are distributed through the Bering, Beaufort, and Chukchi Seas and the Sea of Okhotsk. In the Atlantic, a few hundred bowheads are found in Baffin and Hudson Bays, their associated straits, and along the eastern coast of Greenland as far north as Spitsbergen.

Though an endangered species, bowheads are still hunted by Alaskan Eskimos under a controversial "aboriginal take" quota set each year by the International Whaling Commission (IWC).

bowhead whale

Bryde's Whale

Before the introduction of motorized catcher boats, whalers did not hunt any rorquals because these swift whales could easily outswim any hunters. This and a close resemblance to finbacks explain why Bryde's whales were not identified as a separate species until the early 20th century.

Illustration by Sara Meade

Bryde's Whale (Balaenoptera edeni)

pronounced "Bru'-dess"

Description. Bryde's whales are not as large as some of their fellow rorquals; they reach a maximum length of about 14 m (45 ft) and weigh 27 to 32 metric tons (30 to 35 t). In contrast to the single ridges characteristic of all other baleens, three ridges run down the front of a Bryde's head to the tip of the snout. At close range these ridges give positive identification.

The falcate (sickle-shaped) dorsal fin is about 45 cm (18 in) high and sits two-thirds of the way down the back. The flukes, which are not raised when diving, sometimes seem frayed. Coloration is uniformly dark on Bryde's whales: dark gray skin above and below (including flippers and flukes) and a dark baleen.

Natural History. A Bryde's whale prefers small schooling fish, including mackerel. It will dive deeply in search of food and arch its back high before slipping beneath the surface. Owing to the sharp angle of its swim to the surface, much of the whale's head may appear when it emerges to breathe. This is also characteristic of finbacks and can be an important clue when making an identification at sea. Although it prefers fish, a Bryde's whale will take copepods and krill. It is not, however, a skimmer feeder like the sei whale.

Bryde's whales are often reported approaching boats as if to inspect them, a trait they share with Minke whales and humpbacks.

WHAT TO LOOK FOR

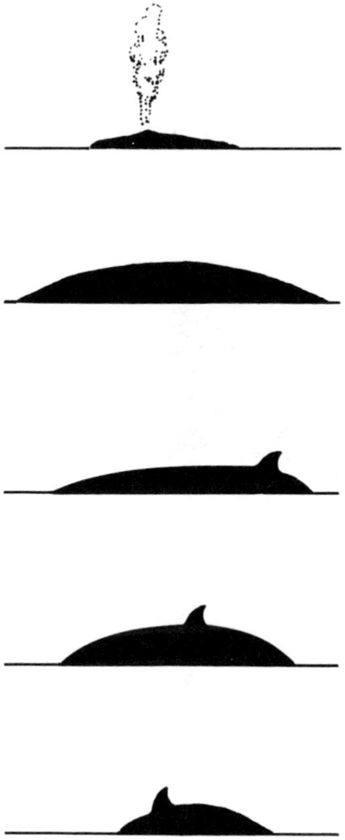

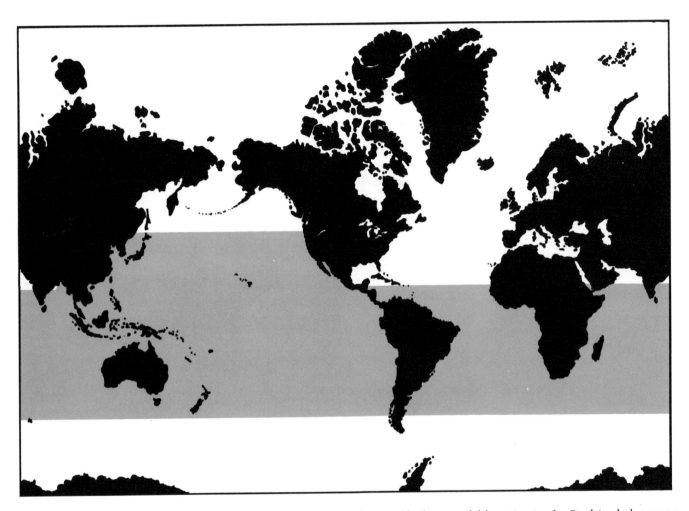

Bryde's whale

Population and Distribution. The best available estimates for Bryde's whales cover only the southern hemisphere and North Pacific. Those populations are thought to total 40,000. Bryde's whales are distributed primarily through highly productive coastal waters in subtropical and tropical latitudes and reportedly range into warm temperate waters. Information on the distribution of Bryde's whales is scanty, based largely on strandings and a few reliable sightings. They are easily mistaken for sei and finback whales, a fact that further confounds efforts to compile an accurate count.

Finback Whale

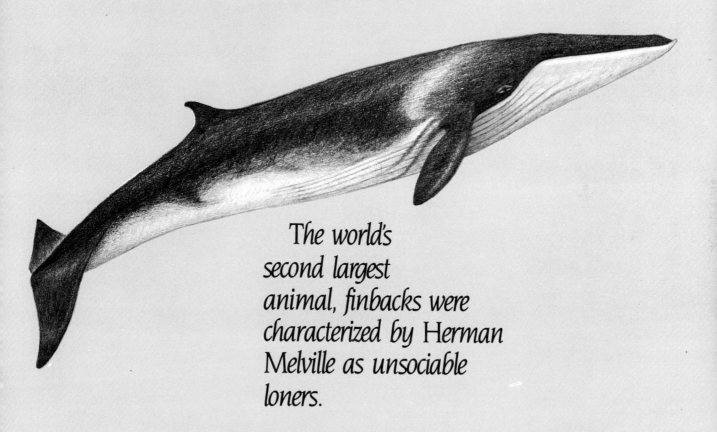

The world's second largest animal, finbacks were characterized by Herman Melville as unsociable loners.

Illustration by Sara Meade

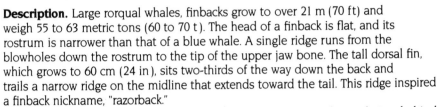

Finback Whale (Balaenoptera physalus)

translation *"fin whale"*

Description. Large rorqual whales, finbacks grow to over 21 m (70 ft) and weigh 55 to 63 metric tons (60 to 70 t). The head of a finback is flat, and its rostrum is narrower than that of a blue whale. A single ridge runs from the blowholes down the rostrum to the tip of the upper jaw bone. The tall dorsal fin, which grows to 60 cm (24 in), sits two-thirds of the way down the back and trails a narrow ridge on the midline that extends toward the tail. This ridge inspired a finback nickname, "razorback."

The finback is dark gray on its sides and back, and white underneath. Just behind the head is a gray-tan chevron, or inverted "V," that points toward the tail; it often is clearly visible when the whale surfaces.

While these markings generally characterize a finback, the most important identifying field mark is the asymmetrical coloration of its head. The left side of the mouth is the same dark gray color as the rest of the body, and the baleen on the left side is dark with some lighter streaks. The lower right jaw and front third of the baleen on the right side, however, are white, and the remainder of the baleen on that side is a dark gray relieved by some light patches. This snowy coloration, visible on approaches from the right, gives a positive identification.

Natural History. Finbacks are omnivorous, with a particular taste for schooling fish, crustaceans, and squid. Though solitary animals, they can occasionally be seen feeding in small groups of two or three, and in areas of heavy food concentration, groups as large as 60 have been reported. Finbacks are sometimes found feeding a kilometer (0.6 mi) or less from shore, but they prefer offshore areas of active upwelling and high productivity. When feeding, finbacks most often turn in a clockwise direction, apparently using the white pigmentation of their right side to school fish or camouflage their approach. Finbacks are not noted for their acrobatics, but they occasionally breach and re-enter the water with a showy splash.

When beginning a deep, dive finbacks arch their backs steeply, which makes the tall dorsal fin more prominent. The tail stock is often raised, as if the flukes were to be lifted from the water, but the whale submerges without exposing its tail. Finbacks are fairly deep divers and have been recorded below 215 m (700 ft). When surfacing at a steep angle from a deep dive, the tip of a finback's rostrum often breaks the water first. This affords a good opportunity to get a clear look at the white jaw and, sometimes, the baleen. A finback is capable of speeds in excess of 20 knots, and often comes almost entirely out of the water when pursuing prey.

As with most whales, finbacks in both hemispheres follow a generally north-south migratory path. The routes are not well understood, but most finbacks seem to abandon their summer feeding grounds and move to more temperate latitudes for the winter months. Mating and calving take place during the winter, and calves are born after a gestation period of about one year.

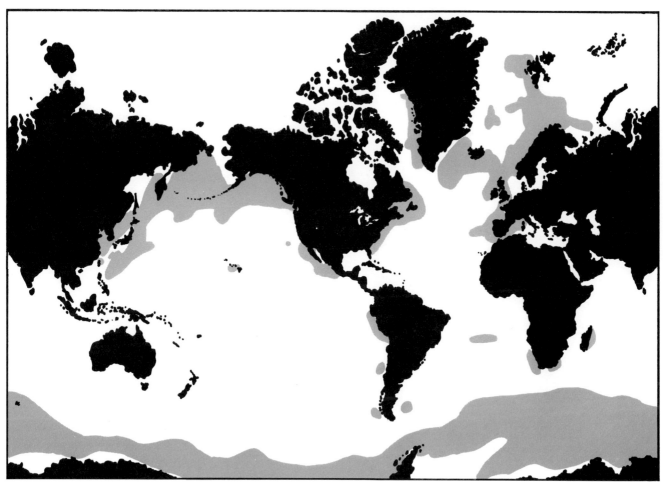

Population and Distribution. There is not enough data to assure an exact count, but the worldwide population is probably close to 100,000. Following the collapse of blue whale stocks, finbacks became a favorite target of the whaling fleets. Fin whales are now hunted only in the North Atlantic by Iceland, Norway and Spain.

Distribution of finback whales is global. Although they live in all oceans, they are uncommon in tropical seas and the high Arctic, preferring temperate waters with abundant food.

finback whale

Gray Whale

Once reduced to a few hundred whales, the dramatic comeback of gray whales symbolizes the hope for conservation efforts worldwide.

Illustration by Sara Meade

Gray Whale (Eschrichtius robustus)

translation: *"fat, robust"*

Description. Another stocky species, gray whales attain lengths of 12 m (40 ft) and weigh about 36 metric tons (40 t). Located on the rear third of the body, a gray whale's dorsal fin is short, nubby, and followed by a line of "knuckles" running down the midline.

As its name suggests, the body, flippers, and flukes of a gray whale are gray with white splotches. The head of a gray is bumpy and warty with bristly facial hairs. Patches of barnacles, algae, and clusters of yellow whale lice cover the rest of the body. Grays breach frequently, perhaps in an effort to dislodge some of this debris. The whales often raise their heads out of the water in a maneuver known as "spyhopping" while migrating along the coastline. Some observers think this is a method for verifying their location. When a gray whale begins a deep dive, it usually raises its flukes into the air.

A gray whale has no more than four throat grooves and a yellow-white baleen that is short and tough. Its slightly bushy blow is about 4 m (12 ft) high.

Natural History. Many gray whales make an annual migration of 6400 kilometers (4000 miles) from summer feeding grounds in the Bering Sea to mating and calving lagoons in Baja California. This is the longest migration made by any mammal, and the northward return trip each spring is a time of particular danger for the new calves, which are occasional targets of orca whales. Gray whales are easily observed from many points along the California coast as they travel between their two homes. They make some vocalizations, and there is evidence that they rely on visual navigation as well.

In the past, the grays' proximity to the coast and their vulnerability in the lagoons and bays of their winter calving grounds made them easy targets for whalers. There were only a few hundred left when the United States, Mexico and the International Whaling Committee (the forerunner of today's International Whaling Commission) granted full protection in the 1930s. By the 1960s, the stock had expanded so dramatically that it spawned a sizable whale-watching industry in California. Grays have recently begun approaching the whale-watching boats, much to the delight of the observers.

Gray whales are bottom feeders, plowing the substrate with their snouts and then straining copepods from the disturbed silt and water. The baleen on the right side is usually more worn than that on the left, indicating that the whales favor their right side when performing this maneuver.

WHAT TO LOOK FOR

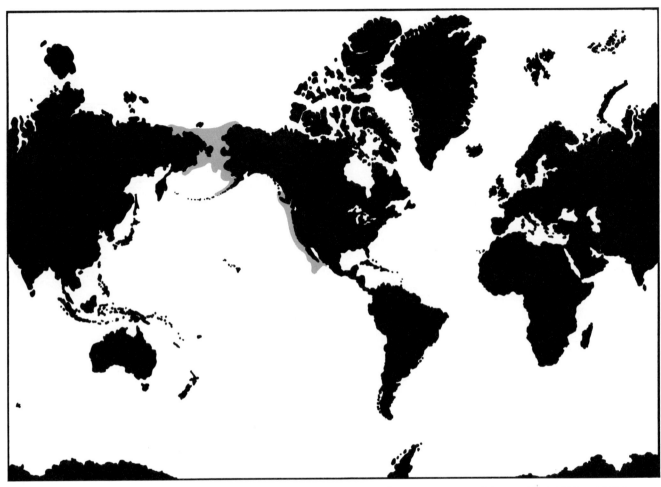

gray whale

Population and Distribution. The vast majority of the world's 14,000 to 18,000 gray whales live in the eastern North Pacific. From a small population off the coast of east Asia and Siberia, the Russians are allowed to take 179 grays annually for distribution to Siberian Eskimos. The Atlantic gray population is assumed to be extinct, since the last sighting occurred in 1775.

Humpback Whale

Humpbacks are probably the world's most popular whales, and certainly its most acrobatic.

Illustration by Sara Meade

Humpback Whale (Megaptera novaeangliae)

translation: *"big-winged New Englander"*

WHAT TO LOOK FOR

Description. Humpback whales, named for the distinctive hump just ahead of the dorsal fin, reach a length of 15.2 m (50 ft) and may weigh 41 metric tons (45 tons). A humpback's body is stout and broad, but not nearly as ungainly as the form most illustrators draw. The skin of a humpback is dark gray/black above, except in the late summer and fall when large patches of light gray old skin may be apparent. The area from the pronounced chin to the belly is usually white, but its color can vary. Fourteen to 30 rorqual grooves stretch from the chin to the belly.

The snout has a single ridge that is all but indistinguishable among the fist-sized knobs covering the face and head. Early whalers called these knobs, which are probably hair follicles, "stovebolts." That name has stuck. The baleen of a humpback whale is dark brown, but in direct sunlight the interior baleen of a feeding humpback can appear almost silver.

Flippers on adult humpbacks measure 4.5 m (15 ft) long, a length matched by no other whale. They inspired the whale's Latinate name, "big winged New Englander." The flippers are slightly scalloped on the leading edge and may be white, dark, or white splashed with black. The dorsal fin, located on the rear third of the back, comes in a variety of shapes, It may be long, hooked over, and seem to dangle in the wind, or it may be short, stubby and look sawed off. Dabs and speckles of white cover many dorsal fins and adjacent areas of the back.

The flukes, each marked with unique black-and-white patterns on its underside, often rise up as a humpback prepares to make a deep dive. The tails are deeply scalloped on the trailing edges. The blow of a humpback whale is bushy and 2.5-3.6 m (8-12 ft) high.

Natural History. Humpbacks sometimes use an ingenious underwater "net" to catch the small schooling fish and krill they like to eat. Diving beneath its prey, a humpback releases enough air to form a circle of bubbles around the fish, frightening them to the surface. The whale then lunges up through the middle of the "net" with its mouth wide open, engulfing thousands of liters of water and fish. To accommodate this huge load, the humpback's throat expands to several times its normal size (the grooves make this possible). The humpback then contracts the muscles in its throat and forces the water out through the baleen, which retain fish and smaller organisms on which it feeds. The long flippers are useful for slapping at schools of fish near the surface, and may be used underwater to "herd" fish into tighter formation. In addition, there is evidence that male humpbacks use their flippers to joust with other males in protecting territorial claims on the breeding grounds. This may explain the scarring and hacking commonly seen on the dorsal fins.

Humpback behavior includes breaching clear of the water; flipper slapping while feeding, resting, or when other whales enter an area; tail slapping and tail breaching, the latter accomplished as the whale throws the rear half of its body out of the water; and "headstands" performed by tail-waving youngsters. Such capering creates the impression that humpbacks are also speedy. They are not: they rarely swim faster than 8-10 knots. Humpbacks are social animals and will remain with the same resting and feeding groups for days. Whales that rest together often divide into new groups for feeding, then return to their original resting groups.

Mating takes place in tropical breeding grounds. Gestation lasts about one year, and the calves nurse for 6-7 months. It is in these breeding grounds that male humpbacks produce their famous, haunting songs. Another noise humpbacks frequently make, one not restricted to the breeding grounds, is a distinctive "elephant roar" when exhaling.

Population and Distribution. The worldwide population of humpback whales is 6500 to 7000. Humpback whales are found in all oceans, and they have standard, distinct north-south migrations. In summer, they are common in certain coastal areas of high productivity. During the winter breeding and calving season, they congregate in tropical waters near islands and coral reefs. Significant seasonal populations are reported off Iceland, Greenland, Labrador, Newfoundland, New England, Alaska, Hawaii, Australia, and in the Antarctic.

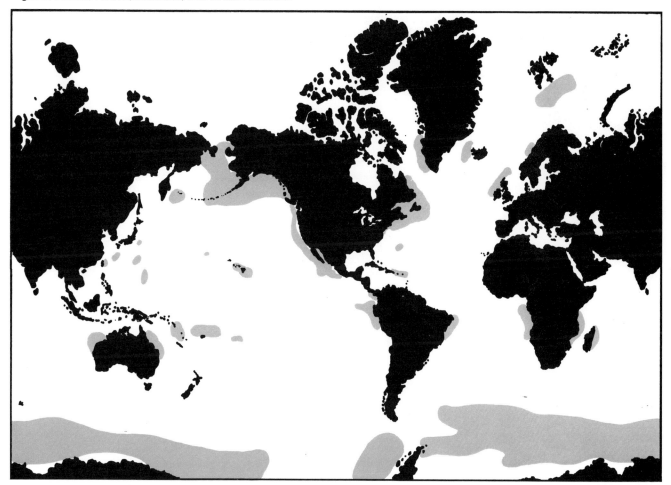

humpback whale

99

Minke Whale

Smallest of the baleen whales, the name commemorates a Norwegian whaler who mistook them for undersized blue whales.

Illustration by Sara Meade

Minke Whale (Balaenoptera acutorostrata)

translation: *"whale with pointed rostrum"*
pronounced "ming-kee"

Description. A Minke is relatively small, but only by cetacean standards. Adults attain a length of 9.1 m (30 ft) and may weigh more than 6.3 metric tons (7 tons). The rostrum of a Minke comes to a point at the tip of the jaws, with a single ridge running from the blowholes to the end of the top jaw.

One of a Minke's distinctive features is a short, sharply curved dorsal fin located on the rear third of its back. Its body, flippers, and flukes are dark on top and white beneath. Minkes of the western North Atlantic have a light gray countershading on their sides. The short baleen plates are a yellowish-white that shade darker toward the back. The blow is so low and light that it is rarely seen.

As a Minke breaks the surface, its pointed snout is often seen clearly, followed by the blowholes and short dorsal fin. When preparing for a deep dive, a Minke arches its back steeply and often shows its tail stock, but it does not raise its flukes when diving.

Natural History. Minke whales prefer schooling fish such as herring, pollock, mackerel, and capelin. In addition, they feed in areas where squid and shrimp are abundant. They travel alone and in groups, but seem to band together most often wherever food is plentiful.

Minkes often enter inlets and bays, coming quite close to shore. It is not unusual for them to approach stationary boats or suddenly appear in front of the bow of a moving vessel. Minkes occasionally breach, leaping clear of the water. Re-entry may be head first and neat, or it may come as a crash landing on the back, a sort of bellyflop in reverse.

In recent years, Minkes have become opportunistic, exploiting food sources left unused by the depleted populations of larger whales.

WHAT TO LOOK FOR

Minke whale

Population and Distribution. The Minke population stands at about 300,000. It is distributed in all oceans worldwide, but is concentrated over shallow cold-water banks of high productivity.

Orca Whale

Perhaps no other animal in the world is as impressive or as feared as an orca whale; few other animals are as misunderstood.

Illustration by Sara Meade

Orca Whale (Orcinus orca)

translation: *"the great killer"*

Description. A male orca reaches a length of 9.1 m (30 ft). A female is smaller, around 8.5 m (28 ft), and has a much slighter build. The dorsal fin, which is the most striking field mark of the species, may reach 2 m (6 ft) in mature males but rarely grows above 1 m (3 ft) in females or immature males.

The body of an orca whale is black above and white below. The area of white extends from the chin to the anal region and reaches upward to the flanks on either side. The undersides of the flukes are white and may be seen during breaching or tailslapping. There are also white oval spots above each eye, and a grayish "saddle" behind the dorsal fin. These color patterns are the rule, but a range of exceptions, running from solid white to solid black, has been reported.

An orca whale has a low, moderately bushy blow.

Natural History. Rarely found swimming alone, orcas are social animals and travel in groups that may include as many as 100 or as few as two. Most commonly, pods of 25 to 35 are observed swimming in close association. Groups may form according to sex and age; females and immature males travel separately from mature males.

Breeding does not appear to be restricted to one season. In the north Pacific, for example, there is evidence that breeding occurs all year, with a peak in early summer. The gestation period lasts at least 13 months, and possibly as long as 16 months. Newborn calves are 2 to 2.4 m (7 to 8 ft) long.

Like other members of the dolphin family, to which orcas belong, these whales are swift and gregarious. They can attain speeds of 25 to 30 knots, and are quite acrobatic, often breaching and spyhopping individually or as a herd.

To maintain their size and high level of activity, orcas require a relatively large caloric intake each day. This appetite has earned them their less-than-savory reputation as "killer" whales. Orcas prefer several species of fish, including tuna, as well as squid and marine birds. But they are also "red meat" eaters and will take seals, porpoises, and even the calves of baleen whales. Few of the scattered but persistent reports of organized attacks on large baleen whales by orcas have been well documented. These whales pose no real threat to humans except in instances when they are provoked or threatened. In oceanariums, orcas have proved to be highly trainable and very gentle. Contrary to the impression produced by some sensationalized reports, "killer" whales do not kill for sport.

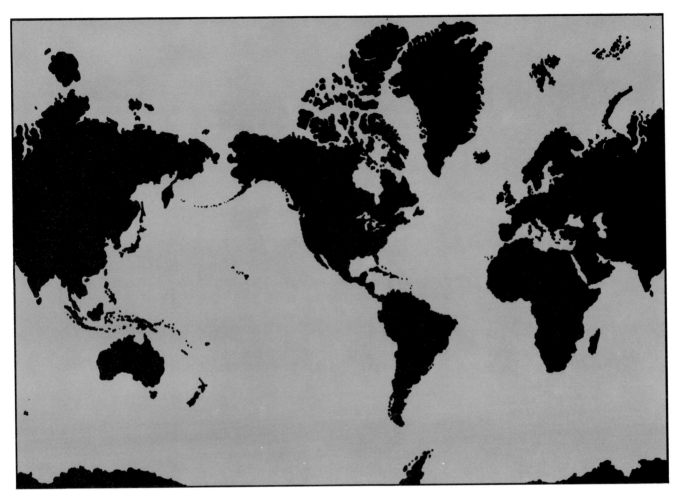

Population and Distribution. The population of orcas is unknown, but they are not thought to be in danger of extinction. They can be found in all oceans but are most common in highly productive colder waters. Orca whales often swim quite close to shore, especially when hunting, and have been seen nearly beaching themselves in pursuit of seals and penguins.

orca whale

Right Whale

Strange-looking right whales were probably the source of many sea monster tales. The name reflects the economics of unmechanized whaling: in the 19th century, abundant oil and valuable byproducts made this the "right" (most profitable) species to kill.

Right Whale (Eubalaena glacialis)

translation: *"true whale in cold water"*

Description. A right whale attains a length of 15 m (50 ft) and may weigh 41 metric tons (45 t). With a stout build that borders on the Rubenesque, a right is extremely slow and rarely exceeds 5 knots when traveling. When hunted, it is capable of 16-knot bursts. It has neither a dorsal fin nor rorqual grooves on its underside. The upper jaw is long, highly arched, and equipped with a 2.1-meter (7-foot) baleen. The distinctive characteristic of the right whale is a pattern of growths called "callosities" scattered over its head and face or wherever facial hair grows on humans. These large growths shelter scores of invertebrates, especially lice (*Cyamus sp.*). The distribution of callosities, also called the "bonnet," is unique to each animal and makes positive identification of individuals possible.

A right's blowholes are set far apart, resulting in a distinct "V"-shaped blow about 4.5 m (12 ft) high. A right's back, baleen, flippers, and flukes are dark, but its stomach and chin are white. The flukes are often raised when it dives.

Natural History. For 19th-century whalers, right whales were inviting targets. Not only did they promise high oil yields and long baleens valuable to manufacturers of clothing, umbrellas, and other products, but the lumbering animals were easy marks for pursuers in unmotorized boats. An extra incentive was the fact that right carcasses do not sink like those of other species. Once extremely important to the economy of many areas — particularly New England — right whales were driven to the edge of extinction by motorized catcher boats and the expansion of the whaling industry.

Rights are coastal whales, often coming into bays and inlets. In the western North Atlantic, they are seen in the Bay of Fundy and offshore on George's Bank. Right whales feed exclusively on copepods and krill, which they strain from the water with their long, fine baleen.

WHAT TO LOOK FOR

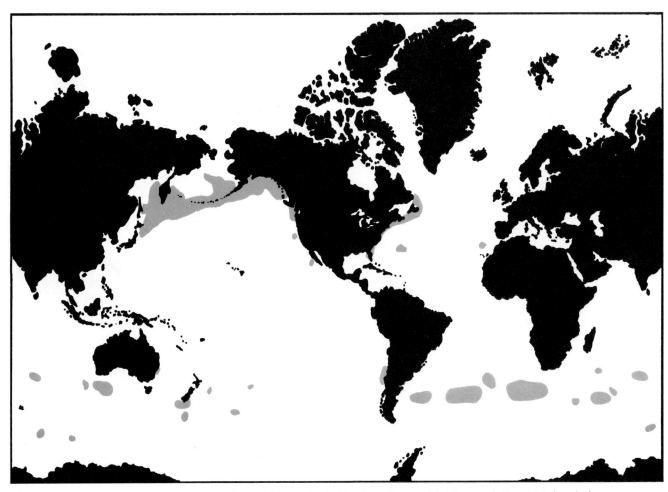

right whale

Population and Distribution. The worldwide population of right whales is approximately 3000. They are sparsely distributed in a few locations in the Indian Ocean, South Pacific, and South Atlantic, particularly along the coast of South Africa. A small population exists off the coast of Patagonia in Argentina. In the northern hemisphere, they are seen in the extreme north of the Pacific between Japan and Alaska, and a small population of perhaps 200 inhabits the western North Atlantic. They are completely protected from commercial whaling by the IWC.

Sei Whale

A large
baleen whale of the
rorqual group. The name
rhymes with "say" and
comes from the Norwegian
word for pollock, large schools
of which often accompany sei
whales.

Illustration by Sara Meade

Sei Whale (Balaenoptera borealis)

translation: *"northern baleen whale"*

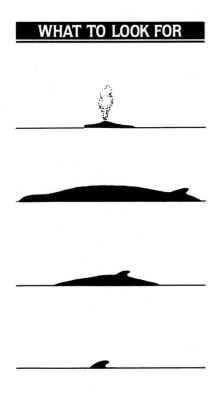

Description. A sei whale reaches a length of 18 m (60 ft) and can weigh over 45 metric tons (50 t). It is dark gray on the back and sides and whitish gray from the chin to the belly, the area of the rorqual grooves. Additional gray/white mottling of the skin appears to be scar tissue from lamprey attacks that occur in warmer waters. The dorsal fin, two-thirds of the way down the whale's back, is falcate and ranges in height from 30 to 60 cm (12 to 24 in). The flippers and flukes are gray, as are the lips and mouth. The baleen is gray with whitish tips.

Between 38 and 56 ventral grooves run along the thorax of a sei whale. These grooves are short in comparison to other rorquals, ending well before the navel. A sei whale has a single head ridge and produces a cone-shaped blow about 4.5 m (15 ft) high.

Natural History. Sei whales are often seen skim-feeding on masses of copepods, a strategy that may throw them into competition with right whales in some regions. When seis feed on schooling fishes they behave more like other rorquals.

A sei whale does not normally execute deep dives, primarily because its favorite foods live in surface waters. As a result, when it returns to the surface from a dive, it is traveling at such a shallow angle that much of its head and back becomes visible at once. When diving, it appears to slip below the surface without lifting its flukes. Again, because its dives are most often shallow, a sei whale rarely arches its back before submerging. When a sei feeds near the surface, its down-times and surface respiration rhythms are persistent and regular; it may travel 91 m (100 yards) or more between surfacings.

Sei whales mate in the winter, and after a one-year gestation period, the mother delivers a 4.5-m (15-ft) calf in the tropical breeding range. The calves nurse for about 7 months and then begin catching their own food.

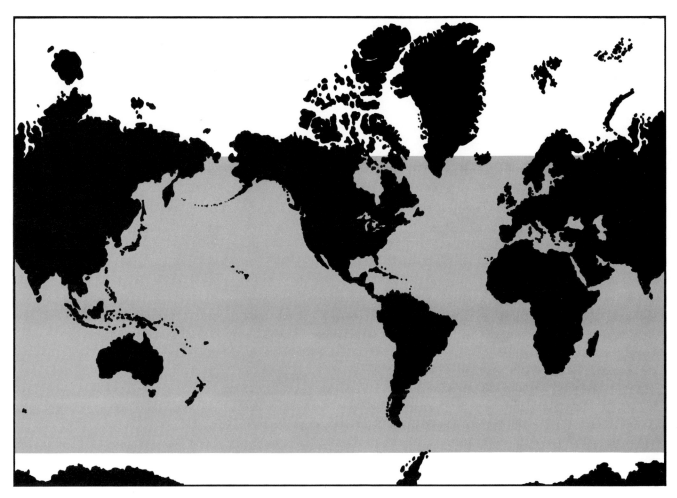

Population and Distribution. Seis number approximately 50,000 to 75,000 worldwide and are found in virtually all tropical and temperate waters. They appear to avoid the pack-ice regions. Their migration periods are poorly understood, but they probably follow a north-south route like most other whale species.

sei whale

Sperm Whale

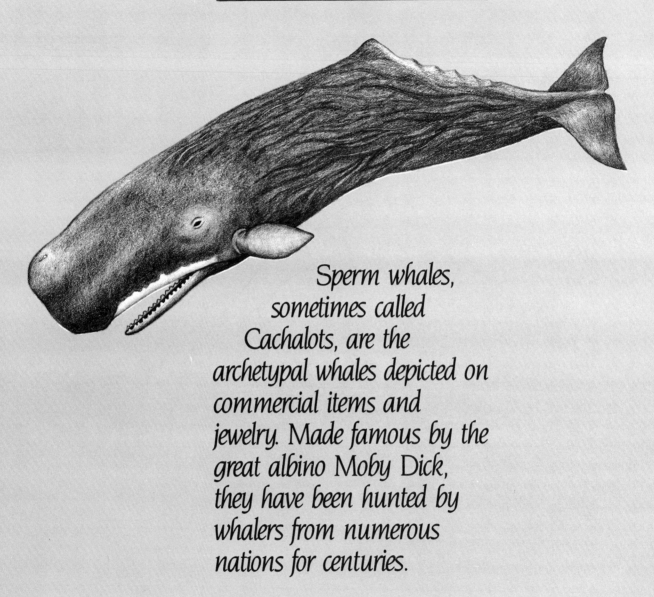

Sperm whales, sometimes called Cachalots, are the archetypal whales depicted on commercial items and jewelry. Made famous by the great albino Moby Dick, they have been hunted by whalers from numerous nations for centuries.

Illustration by Sara Meade

Sperm Whale (Physeter catodon)

translation: *"a blowing toothed whale"*

Description. A male sperm whale can grow to 15.2 m (50 ft) in length, a female to 11 m (35 ft). A sperm whale's outstanding physical feature is a huge, square, oil-rich head that takes up about one-third of its total body length. Positioned on the far left side of the forehead is a prominent blowhole; it produces a low, bushy blow that shoots off to the left at a distinctive 45-degree angle.

The lower jaw is long and narrow, with up to 60 large, conical teeth that were at one time in demand as a favorite medium for scrimshaw. These teeth fit into corresponding sockets in the upper jaw. There are short grooves located along the throat.

A sperm whale's dorsal fin is nothing more than a low hump located two-thirds of the way down the back. Trailing the fin is a row of small, blunt "knuckles." The flukes, raised when diving, are broad, triangular, and notched. The skin of a sperm whale is wrinkled and gives the animal the appearance of having spent too much time in the water. The color is generally a dark brownish-gray, except for a lighter shade of gray on the belly and the front of the head. The corners of the mouth are white, and the undersides of the flukes are dark gray-brown.

Natural History. Sperm whales have been recorded making dives of more than 1070 m (3500 ft) and staying down for more than an hour. Their preferred food is the larger species of squid (giant squid), but they will take octopus and certain fish on occasion. Sperm whales often resurface almost precisely where they began a dive, exhaling loudly when they do. Once resurfaced, they remain in one spot for up to 10 minutes, during which time they may blow as many as 50 times. As with any large whale, the longer the dive, the greater this hyperventilation or "panting" upon resurfacing. Sperm whales prefer deep areas off the continental shelf and are rarely found in waters shallower than 185 m (600 ft).

The waxlike oil called spermaceti that fills a sperm whale's head was once highly valued: candles manufactured from it gave more light than any other kind and were in great demand before the development of electric lighting. In whales, however, the spermaceti serves a different purpose. It solidifies at 0 degrees Celsius (31 Fahrenheit), a water temperature whales only encounter on dives well below the surface of the ocean. Solidification reduces a whale's buoyancy and helps it extend the distance of its dives. As the sperm whale ascends, the spermaceti reliquifies, reducing the energy required for the return.

Sperm whales appear to have a well organized social structure. Groups of 25 to 40 are common, some mixed and some segregated by gender. Lone bulls are sometimes encountered during nonbreeding periods.

WHAT TO LOOK FOR

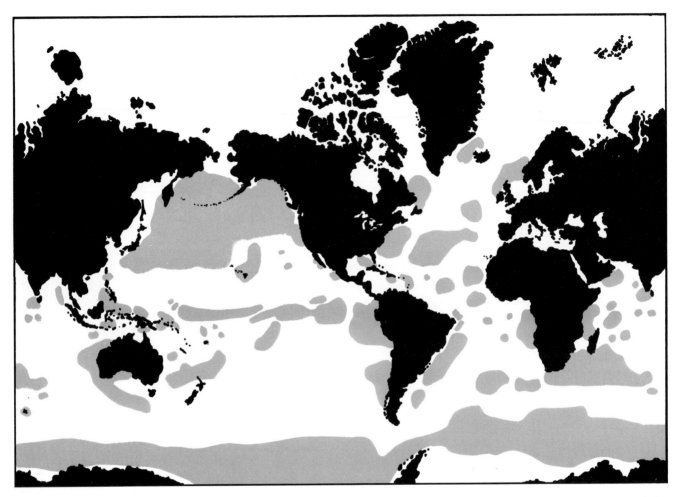

sperm whale

Population and Distribution. The current stock of 600,000 to 700,000 sperm whales is thought to represent about two-thirds of the pre-whaling population. Sperm whales are distributed throughout the temperate, ice-free seas of the world, especially the north and south Pacific and along the eastern and western coasts of South America and Africa. They are also found in several locations in the Indian Ocean, particularly along Australia's western coast. A population of a few thousand exists from the Davis Strait off Labrador, down the eastern U.S. seaboard, and into the Caribbean.

Whale Behaviors

All whales of every size exhibit what are known as "behaviors," or responses to some stimulus or emotion. Many of these behaviors are quite acrobatic; all are exciting to watch. They do not generally occur without specific motivation, and most relate to some larger activity like feeding or navigation.

Listed below are some of the notable behaviors that may be seen while observing whales in the wild. The animals are elusive and totally unpredictable. An observer should be ready for anything when in their company.

Breach: A whale leaps from the water and lands with a splash. In a full breach, the entire body comes out of the water; otherwise, the breach is partial or half. Whales may perform breaches to dislodge barnacles and parasites; humpback whales, for example, may carry over half a ton of parasites on their bodies. Breaching may be a form of communication; when a humpback hits the surface, the sound it produces can be heard for some distance underwater. Breaching may also help move food through the digestive system. A breach may stun fish on which a whale intends to feed, or it may simply be done for the sheer joy of leaping.

Tail Breach: The rear third or half of the whale's body is thrown from the water and slapped down forcefully. This may express pleasure or excitement, or it may serve to produce a noise for communication.

Tail Slap: The tail only is lifted from the water and slapped against the surface, usually repeatedly.

Tail Lob: The tail is lifted from the water and, more gently than in the tail slap, swings back and forth in the air. The whale seems to be standing on its head while doing this.

Flipper Slap: The whale lies on its side or back and repeatedly slaps a flipper against the surface. Generally, only a humpback's flippers are long enough to create a sizable splash in this position. Flipper slaps may be intended for communication or to stun fish near the surface.

Head Stand: The whale is vertical, head down in the water, with the tail stock and flukes straight up in the air. The flukes may wobble slightly.

Spyhop: A whale lifts its head from the water and seems to look around. Because of the lateral location of its eyes, a whale can see ahead only when it is in this position.

Pitchpole: This most often involves orca whales. The whale "stands up" in the water with as much as 80% of its body above the surface. The sight of 30 orcas doing this together is spectacular.

Bibliography

There are many fine books about whales and whaling. This selected bibliography should provide a good starting point for interested readers.

Allen, E. S. 1973. *Children of the Light: The Rise and Fall of New Bedford Whaling and the Death of the Arctic Fleet.* Boston: Little, Brown & Co.

Budker. 1958. *Whales and Whaling.* London: Harrap.

Clark, Colin W. 1976. *Mathematical Bioeconomics.* New York: John Wiley & Sons.

Cousteau, J-Y. and P. Diole. 1975. *Dolphins.* New York: Doubleday.

————. 1972. *The Whale: Mighty Monarch of the Sea.* New York: Doubleday.

Griggs, T., comp. 1975. *There's A Sound In the Sea: A Child's Eye View of the Whale.* San Francisco: Scrimshaw Press.

Haley, Delphine, ed. 1978. *Marine Mammals.* Seattle: Pacific Search Books.

Huntington, G., ed. 1970. *Songs the Whalemen Sang.* New York: Dover.

Katona, S. K., Richardson, D. and R. Hazard. 1972. *The Whales, Dolphins and Porpoises of The Eastern North Pacific: A Guide to Their Identification in the Water.* San Diego Naval Undersea Research Center Rept. No. NUC-TP-282, March.

Lilly J. C. 1975. *Lilly on Dolphins: Humans of the Sea.* New York: Doubleday. Combined revised editions of *Man and Dolphin* and *The Mind of the Dolphin.*

McIntyre, J., comp. 1974. *Mind in the Waters.* New York: Scribner's.

McNulty, F. 1974. *The Great Whales.* New York: Doubleday.

————.1975. *Whales: Their Life in the Sea.* New York: Harper & Row.

Matthews, L. H., ed. 1968. *The Whale.* New York: Simon and Schuster.

Melville, H. *Moby Dick.* Any edition.

Mowat, F. 1972. *A Whale for the Killing.* Boston: Atlantic-Little, Brown.

Murphy, R. C. 1967. *A Dead Whale or A Stove Boat.* Boston: Houghton Mifflin.

Norris, K. S., ed. *Whales, Dolphins and Porpoises.* Berkeley: University of California Press.

Pryor, K. 1975. *Lads Before the Wind: Adventures in Porpoise Training.* New York: Harper & Row.

Robertson, R. B. 1954. *Of Whales and Men.* New York: Knopf.

Sanderson, Ivan T. 1961. *Follow the Whale.* New York: Bramhall House.

Scammon, C. M. 1968 (1874). *The Marine Mammals of the North-Western Coast of North America, Together with an Account of the American Whale-Fishery.* New York: Dover.

Scheffer, V. B. 1969. *The Year of the Whale.* New York: Scribner's

Schevill, W. E., ed. 1973. *The Whale Problem.* Cambridge: Harvard University Press.

Slipjer, E. J. 1962. *Whales.* New York: Basic Books.

Small, G. L. 1971. *The Blue Whale.* New York: Columbia University Press.

Stackpole, E. A. 1972 (1953). *The Sea-Hunters: New England Whalemen During Two Centuries, 1635-1835.* Westport, CT: Greenwood Press.